CW00616977

# HOW
## IS
# BRITAIN?

HUTCHINSON RADIUS

# HOW GREEN IS BRITAIN?

Friends of the Earth

Hutchinson Radius
London Sydney Auckland Johannesburg

Hutchinson Radius
An imprint of Random Century Ltd
20 Vauxhall Bridge Road, London SW1V 2SA

Random Century Australia (Pty) Ltd
20 Alfred Street, Milsons Point
Sydney NSW 2061, Australia

Random Century (NZ) Ltd
9 Rothwell Avenue, Albany, Auckland 10
New Zealand

Random Century South Africa (Pty) Ltd
PO Box 337, Bergvlei, 2012 South Africa

First published by Hutchinson Radius 1990

British Library Cataloguing in Publication Data
Porritt, Jonathan
How Green is Britain : the government's environmental
record.
1. Great Britain. Environment. Policies of government
I. Title  II. Secrett, Charles

ISBN 0 –09–174598–5

Photoset by Speedset Ltd, Ellesmere Port, South Wirral
Printed and bound in Great Britain by
Mackays of Chatham, Chatham, Kent
ISBN 0 09 1745985

Printed on 100% recycled paper

# Contents

# Acknowledgements

This book has its origins in two earlier Friends of the Earth Reports, *The Environment: The Government's Record*, published in February 1989, and an update of that report, *The Government's Environmental Record 1979-1989*, produced at the end of 1989. That edition has been substantially rewritten and brought up-to-date again, and includes consideration of the Government's first ever comprehensive White Paper on the Environment, *This Common Inheritance*. Throughout these editions, so many people have made contributions that we cannot list them all, but rather thank them collectively. Special thanks, however, are due to Jonathon Porritt and Charles Secrett, the co-authors of the original Report. Jonathon was Director of Friends of the Earth until June 1990, and Charles was formerly Campaigns Coordinator. It was Charles' major effort of research and writing that crystallised the original version into one book from the ideas and drafts of many.

Particular thanks are also due to Environmental Data Services Limited, whose monthly 'ENDS Report' is regularly read by the campaigners at Friends of the Earth. 'The ENDS Report' is an excellent digest of news on environmental issues and the legal and regulatory background, and makes an invaluable contribution to sources of reference at Friends of the Earth. Some of the information in this book originated in articles from 'The ENDS Report', and we thank the editor and his colleagues for permission to use the material.

# Introduction

In 1988, the Planet sent powerful signals to people and politicians, which few could ignore. There were droughts in the USA and China; floods in Bangladesh; an alarmingly large hole in the ozone layer was identified above Antarctica; and 1988 was also the fifth year of the 1980s of record-high temperatures. An international conference of scientists and politicians described the consequences of climate change as 'second only to a global nuclear war'.

Mrs Thatcher was one of the first World leaders to respond to these signals with her speech on the environment to the Royal Society on September 27th 1988. Her rhetoric was impressive. 'We might have begun', she said, 'a massive experiment with the system of this planet itself.' She echoed the conclusions of the 1987 United Nations Brundtland Report *Our Common Future* by recognising that 'the health of the economy and the health of our environment are totally dependent upon each other.'

A few weeks later, in October 1988, she told the Annual Conference of her party that Conservatives were 'not merely friends of the Earth, but its guardians and trustees for generations to come.' On November 8th 1989, she told the UN Assembly that it is 'mankind and his activities which are changing the environment of our Planet in damaging and dangerous ways . . . the evidence is there . . . the damage is being done.'

With these three speeches, Mrs Thatcher has done more to push environmentalism to the top of the political, business and economic agendas both here and abroad than any other politician, although Mikhail Gorbachev has not been far behind. She has certainly come a long way since she confessed that she found her experiences as a Junior Minister at the Department of the Environment in the 1970s as somewhat 'humdrum'.

However, her conversion is, as yet, largely confined to the realm of rhetoric. One year after seeing the green light, a leader in the *Financial Times* said of Mrs Thatcher that her

> public conversion to the environmental cause came during her tenth year of office, while that of the Government as a whole has yet to be completed. Mrs Thatcher remains out of tune with deepening green opinion on . . . nuclear power . . . the car . . . and the nature and extent of economic growth. (*Financial Times*, November 8th 1989.)

At the end of 1990, despite the Environmental Protection Act and the promised White Paper on the environment, Mrs Thatcher and her Government remain out of step with the deepening environmental crisis.

This report shows that whilst there have been some welcome recent improvements, the record taken as a whole is very poor. Our analysis describes the problems and sets the scene for what needs to be done. The detailed sections below amply demonstrate that the claims made by Nicholas Ridley when he was Secretary of State for the Environment, that 'Britain has taken the lead' on the environment, were absurd.

On key environmental commitments which have come through EC directives rather than domestic initiatives such as pollution from power stations and small cars, the Government has been a reluctant and belated convert. Although Mrs Thatcher has announced increased aid for tropical rainforests and climate research, her Ministers have not supported other countries' recent proposals on targets and timetables to deal with the urgent issues of ozone depletion and global warming.

Politicians cannot claim that environmentalism is not popular. The Department of the Environment's own survey in 1989 showed the depth and breadth of public anxiety over pollution. All classes were 'worried' about chemicals in rivers and the sea (91%), traffic fumes (74%), tropical rainforest destruction (76%), destruction of the ozone layer (83%), and loss of trees and hedgerows (72%). Surveys also show that the public is prepared to act, through green consumerism, and to pay for environmental protection and improvement, through, for example, higher prices or taxes on energy.

The spectacularly successful consumer boycott of aerosol sprays containing ozone-damaging chemicals, which Friends of the Earth led in 1988 with its publication *The Aerosol Connection*, convinced manufacturers to act without them waiting for government intervention. When green consumers insist on pesticide residue testing and the labelling of products, they are promoting freedom of information, questioning the safety of pesticides which miss the pest target and end up in food or drinking water, and raising the demand for pesticide-free and organically grown food. Part of our work at Friends of the Earth is to sound alarm bells about such problems and support the public in being a force for change.

Individual action by citizens or corporations is limited, however. In many areas of pollution control and environmental protection, government action and regulation is essential. For competitive industries, the need to minimise their costs by, for example, discharging gases to the air or waste to the river or landfill site, without calculating the cost to the community, can only be removed by persuading all companies to stop polluting. As corporate leaders keep telling us, they need the 'level playing field' which regulation of the market place brings. An unfettered market cannot deal with pollution. Long-term planning, domestic and international regulations and agreements, as well as financial incentives such as taxes, subsidies, incentives, grants and permits, are all essential if the Planet is to get the protection it requires. Mrs Thatcher is now struggling to adapt to these new political imperatives of environmentalism, which are in stark contrast to the deregulation and individualism that she has promoted during the 1980s. This is why we have had two years of discordance between her green words and actions – a green credibility gap which is separating the public from the politicians.

A major chance to close this gap was missed. The 1990 White Paper, *This Common Inheritance*, which Environment Minister Chris Patten had said would 'define the orientation of our environmental policies into the next century', was mainly a disappointing reiteration of current politices. More optimistically, we note that the exercise may have sown the seeds for greening of the government machine. The Cabinet-level committee established to coordinate the production of the White Paper will remain to consider environmental policies, and within each government Department, a Minister with responsibilities for environmental matters will be appointed.

Such steps do not, of course, guarantee worthwhile changes. The publication of the White Paper itself was a depressing example of political compromise. Most of the 350 initiatives, very few of which constitute new proposals, represent only minor readjustments to the political and legislative framework for environmental protection. It would appear that the Treasury has scotched any attempt to promote the radical policies which the Planet now needs. Opposition from Transport, Energy and Agricultural Ministers seems to have prevented significant action on key causes of environmental damage. Earlier suggestions of an overhaul of environmental economics have been diluted, and the discussion relegated to an Annex of the White Paper.

The green credibility gap is wider than ever, as the short-term views of politicians reflect the power of vested interests and conflict with the long-term needs of the Planet and her people. Time is running out. The latest scientific evidence on the ozone layer and on global warming has been described by the scientists themselves as 'horrifying' and 'alarming'. Mrs Thatcher's latest speech on global warming concluded that 'the repair work needs to start without delay'.

Mrs Thatcher can place her stamp indelibly on the history of the Planet if she soon marks the last decade of this millenium with specific targets and timetables on energy efficiency, greenhouse gas reductions, protection of the ozone layer, pollution controls and resources for the Third World. If she does not take this lead, then the children of the next millenium will never forgive her. We hope that our report will provide the spur to this action.

David Gee
Director
Friends of the Earth
October 1990

# Chapter 1

# A DEEP BREATH: AIR POLLUTION

The sky over London in the first few days of May 1990 provided dramatic visible evidence of the pollution of our air. A succession of sunny, still days had produced ideal conditions for the build-up of 'photochemical smog', the haze of toxic chemicals – including oxides of nitrogen, hydrocarbons, and ozone – which was first identified over Los Angeles and which now regularly blurs the skies over Athens, London and many other big cities.

Vehicle exhaust is one major source of pollutants, involving hundreds of different chemicals. Nitrogen oxides (nitric oxide and nitrogen dioxide) are formed in engines by the combination of either atmospheric nitrogen or nitrogen in the petrol with oxygen. Nitrogen oxides and hydrocarbons (unburnt and partly burnt fuel) combine in strong sunlight to form ozone. Ozone in the upper atmosphere is an essential shield against harmful solar rays, but at ground level it is toxic. It can cause severe breathing difficulties for people with chest ailments, and it also adversely affects plant growth. The sooty particles from diesel engine emissions may be linked with cancer.

Power stations are another major source of air pollution. Sulphur dioxide ($SO_2$) and oxides of nitrogen ($NO_x$) are the main gases which react with water in the atmosphere to form acid rain. (And, as outlined in the section on Global

Warming below, carbon dioxide from fossil fuel burning is a major 'greenhouse gas'.)

A third threat to the atmosphere comes from CFCs (chlorofluorocarbons) and other ozone-destroying chemicals. These chemicals eat into the beneficial ozone layer in the upper atmosphere. Action is finally being taken to ban most uses of CFCs in the form of a recently revised international agreement, but the dates set by governments are tardy, and the agreement does not cover all ozone-depleting chemicals. The British Government's national response has been belated and inadequate. The problems are widely recognised, but we are still waiting for the necessary action to halt production and use of all 'ozone depleters'. Major uses for such chemicals still include refrigeration units, fire extinguishers and foam insulation materials.

# Acid rain

Acid rain is a term used to describe a cocktail of atmospheric pollutants. The main pollutants are sulphur dioxide and nitrogen oxides. Their main effects are to cause damage to forests, rivers, lakes and buildings. The 1988 House of Commons Environment Committee, which considered air pollution and acid rain, received 'deeply disturbing evidence' of damage to stonework and stained glass at places including Westminster Abbey, Lincoln Cathedral, York Minster, Beverley Minster, Brompton Oratory, St Paul's Cathedral, Westminster Palace and Liverpool Cathedral. The architect to Beverley Minster told the Committee that 'many of our most valuable stone buildings are now suffering from accelerating decay of their most characteristic features. In many cases exquisite and often irreplaceable medieval craftsmanship, which has endured for centuries, is literally disintegrating before our eyes.'

Forests throughout Europe have been affected, and in Norway and Sweden thousands of lakes are devoid of fish life as a result of acid rain. Most expert scientists agree that if we are to protect forest and freshwater ecosystems from acid rain damage, massive cuts in emissions of sulphur dioxide and nitrogen oxides are required. Existing UK policy comes nowhere near meeting this goal.

Government estimates have shown that British sulphur dioxide emissions totalled 3.66 million tonnes in 1988, with 71 per cent coming from power stations. At 2.5 million tonnes, nitrogen oxide emissions were the second highest loads recorded since the early seventies. Thirty-two per cent of $NO_x$ is from power stations and 45 per cent from vehicles, so as demand for electricity and cars grows, levels will rise – unless firm action is taken. But Britain has consistently dragged its feet.

In 1986, under mounting pressure from Norway and Sweden, the UK announced a programme to fit three existing large power stations with pollution control devices to remove sulphur, known as flue gas desulphurisation (FGD) equipment. Four years later there are still no power stations operating with FGD in place. Construction of desulphurisation equipment has begun at Drax power station in Yorkshire, but it is not expected to begin operation until the end of 1993. Britain's well-earned 'dirty man of Europe' nickname has been difficult to shake off – and with good reason. West Germany began its clean-up programme in 1984, and other countries such as the Netherlands, France, Sweden, Austria, and Finland all have FGD installations. Britain still has not joined the '30 per cent club' of European nations aiming for a minimum 30 per cent cut in sulphur dioxide emissions by 1993.

Exactly the same has been happening with nitrogen oxides. In November 1988, we refused to join with other countries aiming at 30 per cent cuts, merely agreeing instead to a freeze at current levels under the UN Economic

3

Commission for Europe's $NO_x$ protocol. The Central Electricity Generating Board (CEGB) has a programme to install special burners to reduce the production of nitrogen oxides at existing plants. This is a welcome step, but it will cut $NO_x$ power station emissions by an average of only 30 per cent – and power stations, we have seen, account for only about one-third of the total.

The British Government's attitude has been repeatedly criticised both at home and abroad. The 1988 House of Commons Environment Committee reported that the CEGB was spending less than £200,000 per year on research in desulphurisation technology, and had even refused permission for a company to install a large pilot plant at an existing power station. The Committee concluded that the lack of research in Britain would either 'lengthen the timescale or force the use of foreign technology', and recommended that 'further encouragement' be given to research, including grants from the Department of Trade and Industry. The Government, in its response to the Committee's recommendations, made no such promise.

The UK produces more sulphur dioxide than any other EEC country, yet for four years Britain blocked the proposed EC Directive on emissions from large combustion plants (such as coal-burning electricity plants), and rejected a series of compromises on emission targets. In mid-1988, this policy drew scathing criticisms from other European governments. The British attitude was 'totally unreasonable', complained the Belgians in 1988, while the Netherlands deplored attempts to impose a 'British diktat' on the discussions.

Finally, at the June 1988 EEC Environment Ministers' Council, the UK accepted compromise targets. The sulphur dioxide targets were agreed as a result of special pleading by the UK. Two points were stressed: the need to protect the coal industry – British coal has a higher sulphur content and the importation of low sulphur coal could have

4

damaged the domestic industry – and the inability to introduce FGD equipment quickly enough. As a result, Britain's sulphur dioxide reduction targets were set lower than those for most other countries, including the German Federal Republic. For large power stations (over 50 megawatts) the agreed targets were a 20 per cent cut by 1993, 40 per cent by 1998, and 60 per cent by 2003.

In September 1989, the Government published its proposals to implement the Large Combustion Plant Directive. Twelve thousand megawatts of generating capacity were to be fitted with FGD equipment in order to achieve the necessary reductions in sulphur dioxide emissions, at a cost of about £2 billion. Right up until the end of 1989, the Prime Minister was boasting about the size of the acid rain clean-up programme: 'With regard to energy, we already have a £2 billion programme to reduce acid rain emissions from our power stations.' The FGD programme was also confirmed by Environment Minister David Trippier in December 1989.

However, the Government's commitment to pollution control has proved no match for its desire to privatise the electricity industry. Energy Secretary John Wakeham announced a drastic reduction in the desulphurisation programme in April 1990, saying he expected de-sulphurisation equipment to be fitted at only 8,000 megawatts worth of plant, at a cost of £1.2 billion. The remainder of the sulphur dioxide reduction targets would be met by other measures 'including switching to low sulphur fuels'. This revised programme blatantly ignores the fact that the UK was set particularly lenient targets by the EC partly because we insisted that higher targets could not be met without the use of imported low sulphur fuels. Having broken its original promise, and hence the spirit of the EC agreement, the Government shows few signs of making amends by accepting the higher reduction targets set for other countries. Britain will remain the largest producer of sulphur dioxide in Western Europe.

The UK was also given lax nitrogen oxide targets: 15 per cent cuts by 1993 and 30 per cent by 1998, instead of the 20 and 40 per cent cuts set for Belgium, France, the Netherlands, Luxembourg, and West Germany.

The sad truth is that all these agreements, even if they were fully implemented, fall far short of what is needed. The Swedish Government has reckoned that sulphur deposits need to be cut by 70 per cent in the south-west of Sweden to halt soil acidification. The UK Government's own scientists have shown that a 90 per cent cut in acid deposition would be required to restore certain sensitive UK waters to near pristine condition.

# Vehicle exhausts and public health

Catalytic converters fitted to exhaust systems of vehicles can reduce the three major pollutants, nitrogen oxides, hydrocarbons and carbon monoxide, by up to 90%. The exhaust fumes then contain nitrogen (an inert gas which already forms about 80% of our air), water vapour, and the greenhouse gas, carbon dioxide. By the end of 1992, compulsory fitting of catalytic converters will begin to soften the impact of petrol exhaust fumes from new cars. However, if the Government's own forecasts of the increase in road traffic by 2025 (between 83 and 142 per cent) prove correct, any beneficial effect of catalytic converters could quickly be cancelled out. At worst, the emissions of nitrogen oxides from road traffic may be higher in 2020 than today, despite their introduction.

As many as five million new vehicles may be sold in this country before the fitting of catalytic converters becomes compulsory. Moreover, the Government's White Paper on the Environment (*This Common Inheritance*, September 1990) notes that cars less than three years old account for almost half the car mileage in the UK. Friends of the Earth research has shown that significant improvements in air quality could be achieved if the Government offered financial incentives to encourage the use of catalytic converters. Fitting these to new cars two years ahead of the legal deadline, and to cars which are three years old or less, would cut car exhaust emissions by 31% for hydrocarbons, 27% for carbon monoxide, and 22% for nitrogen oxides over a fourteen year period. West Germany offers subsidies to encourage use of catalytic converters, both for new and old cars. Yet no action has been taken by the UK Government on this issue.

Furthermore, catalytic converters do not remove all pollutants. The only current method to reduce carbon dioxide, a major greenhouse gas, from vehicle emissions, is to reduce fuel consumption. But there are no fuel efficiency requirements for vehicles and no vehicle emission limits for carbon dioxide in Britain today.

Diesel engines have sometimes been seen as 'cleaner' than petrol engines, because the fuel does not need lead additives, and the engines generally emit less gaseous pollutants. However, they emit much higher levels of black smoke, or particulates. These particulates make buildings dirty, and are responsible for the smell associated with diesel engine exhausts. The particulates carry other substances like heavy metals and complex organic materials, such as polyaromatic hydrocarbons, some of which have the potential to cause cancer. Diesel fuel has long been favoured in Britain for heavy goods vehicles and public transport. Because these vehicles are often badly maintained, their exhaust fumes may contain higher quantities of pollutants. A programme to fit special exhaust filters to buses would do much to reduce air pollution in urban areas, but the Government has no plans for this. The present UK standard for diesel Heavy Goods Vehicles (HGVs) is unscientific and inadequate, involving a visual estimate of

7

the blackness of the smoke. Friends of the Earth has been campaigning for US emission standards for HGVs. The British Government has now accepted that US standards should apply. However, implementation of the standards will depend on adoption of the limits throughout the EEC which will probably delay this urgent improvement.

Vehicle emissions of nitrogen oxides help cause acid rain. On top of this, the public health dangers of ozone, carbon monoxide and other exhaust products are well known. Ozone can irritate the lungs, eyes, nose and throat, and cause headaches. Carbon monoxide deprives the body of oxygen by interfering with the red blood cells. Nitrogen oxides can also harm lungs, leading to bronchitis and pneumonia. Lead is a highly toxic metal, and it can affect the development of the nervous system in children.

A Friends of the Earth study, welcomed by the British Heart Foundation and the British Lung Foundation, has shown that as many as one person in five faces health risks through air pollution. Those susceptible include the elderly, pregnant women, children under 2 years old, and people suffering from illnesses such as asthma, bronchitis, emphysema and angina.

In early 1988, the Government's own Warren Spring Laboratory reported that the World Health Organization's (WHO) air quality guidelines for ozone and sulphur dioxide are widely exceeded in Britain. And at a number of sites, excessive levels of atmospheric lead, cadmium and nitrogen dioxide are likely to be found.

Alarmingly, the Government has been reluctant to inform the public of such problems. During the three month period between October and December 1988, carbon monoxide levels exceeded the WHO guideline on 24 days at one London site alone. The highest reading was almost double the WHO guideline. During the hot summers of 1989 and 1990, WHO's ozone guideline levels were regularly topped. The Government had to be pressed repeatedly by Friends of the Earth before the Department of the Environment (DoE) agreed to make information available – but only on request. Finally, in September 1990, the Government went a stage further and promised to include such information in weather bulletins. However, the Government will not grant powers to local authorities to shut down factories or curb car use in an emergency as happens in some other countries.

UK Government monitoring of nitrogen dioxide is unsatisfactory, too. The EC Directive on air quality standards for nitrogen dioxide recommends monitoring at the 'hot spots' where levels are most likely to build up. But in one case, the monitoring site is tucked away in a back street. Friends of the Earth research in 1989 suggested that levels had been breached, and it called on the European Commission to investigate.

# Lead in petrol

At last, the Government can claim to be promoting lead-free petrol. In 1987, the Chancellor cut the duty on unleaded fuel to bring it into line with leaded, and in 1988 unleaded was five to six pence per gallon cheaper. In 1989, the Government fulfilled an EC Directive requiring it to encourage the use of unleaded petrol: a substantial price differential, ten to twelve pence per gallon, was created, and over £1 million was spent on a Government publicity campaign.

All this was a tardy response to a mixture of public anxiety, European law, and pressure from CLEAR (the Campaign for Lead-Free Air) and from the Government's own advisers. The Royal Commission on Environmental Pollution had strongly recommended such action as early as 1983. Far from setting the environmental pace, the Government had to be dragged to the starting-line.

# Ozone depletion and CFCs

'The United Kingdom is leading the world in the efforts to save the ozone layer,' said David Trippier, Minister for the Environment, in January 1990. The Government is willing to lead the field in terms of 'green' rhetoric, but unfortunately that is about as far as it goes.

In May 1989 Britain joined more than 80 other countries in calling for the phasing out of CFCs – chlorofluorocarbons, identified as major culprits in damaging the earth's protective ozone shield. But the way was paved by consumer pressure and media coverage, largely generated by Friends of the Earth campaigns. As recently as 1987, the Department of the Environment was lobbying only for a freeze at current levels. Then, in 1988, the leading aerosol and fast food manufacturers and retailers announced that they would stop using CFCs. Where Friends of the Earth had led, industry followed, and the Government tagged along behind.

The Government now claims that it is ten years ahead of schedule in meeting the goals of the 1987 Montreal Protocol, an international agreement which sets chemical reduction targets to protect the ozone layer. However the large drop in CFC use is easy to explain. Levels fell rapidly, because a staggering 64 per cent of the UK total had been used in aerosol spray cans, and substitutes were readily available.

Unfortunately, the ozone layer is still threatened. Even without CFCs, other chemicals remain in production which damage it. Some, ironically, are being marketed as CFC substitutes. These other ozone-depleting chemicals include HCFCs (hydrochlorofluorocarbons), which industry estimates may take up to 30% of the current demand for CFCs; halons, used mainly in fire extinguishers; methyl chloroform, used in industrial metal cleaning operations; and carbon tetrachloride, which is used in the production of

CFCs. The Government is dragging its feet over controlling them.

Other countries such as West Germany have set a programme for the total phase-out of CFCs and a number of other ozone-depleting chemicals by 1995. Why can't Britain follow suit? West Germany and Sweden will ban all CFCs from use in the electronics industry in January 1991, but in Britain many companies stubbornly resist change, secure in the knowledge that Britain is not going to legislate. We are still waiting, too, for compulsory labelling and recycling schemes to be introduced for products containing CFCs and other ozone-depleting chemicals. There is also a lack of disposal schemes for the CFCs in domestic fridges, even though the industry itself has been calling for their introduction.

*Friends of the Earth Policy Recommendations*

## Air Pollution

Rather than relying on industry voluntarily reducing air pollution levels or settling for weakened emission controls, the following measures are needed to ensure cleaner air for all.

**1.** The Government should set emission standards for power stations that would not harm natural eco-systems. Sulphur dioxide and nitrogen oxide emissions should be reduced by 75 per cent by 1995, and 90 per cent as soon as possible.

**2.** The Government should introduce the US 1994 emission standards for diesel trucks on a similar timescale to the US, and introduce US 1987 emission standards for diesel cars as soon as possible. A

11

programme to fit filters to remove particulate matter from bus exhaust fumes should be introduced.

**3.** Tax incentives should be used to encourage speedy introduction of catalytic converters and to discourage the use of more polluting vehicles.

**4.** The tax subsidy for company cars should be abolished at the next budget. *[Reiterated as 'Transport' Policy Recommendation #3, 'Global Warming' Policy Recommendation #5]*

**5.** Car use should be controlled by building up public transport, to prevent gains from pollution control being wiped out by the increase in the number of cars. *[Reiterated as 'Global Warming' Policy Recommendation #6]*

**6.** The Government should implement a national programme to phase out the production and consumption of ozone-damaging CFCs, halons and methyl chloroform (with the vast majority going by 1992, bar essential medical uses and some existing refrigeration use); and confine HCFC use to essential applications and set an early phase out date. *[Reiterated as 'Global Warming' Policy Recommendation #9]*

**7.** Compulsory labelling and recycling schemes for products that still contain CFCs should be introduced. The Government should also levy a 'polluter pays' tax from CFC producers to raise funds for technology transfer to help developing countries to meet their needs without using CFCs. *[Reiterated as 'Global Warming' Policy Recommendation #10]*

**8.** The Government should set up a smog 'alert' system, giving local authorities powers to reduce elevated levels of pollution by closing down factories and controlling vehicle use during pollution episodes.

**9.** The World Health Organization air quality guidelines for Europe should be adopted as statutory air quality standards.

# Chapter 2

# FIT TO DRINK? WATER POLLUTION

May 3$^{rd}$ 1990: a biologist at the University of Essex identified the toxic chemicals PCBs (polychlorinated biphenyls) as being one of the main reasons for the disappearance of otters from six rivers in East Anglia. On a seventh Norfolk river, the Wissey, the biologist found a declining otter colony in a 'precarious position'. PCB levels in dung collected from these animals were the highest ever recorded in British otters. PCBs are used in certain electrical equipment. When they are released into the environment they build up in the fatty tissues of aquatic mammals and may decrease reproduction rates. PCBs are also suspected of causing cancer.

May 6$^{th}$ 1990: the National Rivers Authority sounded the alarm over blooms of toxic algae again growing in inland waters. In 1989, 35 sheep and dogs died after contact with toxic algae in Rutland Water and further checks showed that 53 lakes and reservoirs were affected. By June 1990, these types of algal blooms had appeared in 72 waters in England and Wales.

May 31$^{st}$ 1990: Massive publicity accompanied reports that the European Commission is to take Britain to the European Court of Justice over sewage contamination of bathing waters at Blackpool, Formby and Southport. Friends of the Earth released Government documents showing that it tried to postpone a prosecution until after privatisation of the water industry. Soon after, the European Commission announced its intention to take action over the failure of another 134 British beaches to meet the EEC's legal standards during 1988. Meanwhile in northeast England, a ban was slapped on shellfish sales as toxic algae built up in the seawater.

All is very far from well in Britain's seas and rivers.

# The North Sea: Britain's record of shame

North Sea pollution is documented in annual reports by two international bodies: the Oslo Commission and the Paris Commission. During the 1980s, they have recorded alarming levels of waste disposal: burning of hazardous wastes, dumping of sludges and wastes from sewage treatment and from the chemical and pharmaceutical industries, spillage and disposal of oil from drilling platforms, and thousands of tonnes of chemicals pouring in from rivers. 1.7 million tonnes of liquid industrial waste, 2 million tonnes of solid industrial waste and 30,000 tonnes of oil were dumped or spilled into the North Sea in 1988 alone.

Britain's record on the North Sea has not been a proud one and the Government's authorisation of sewage sludge dumping in the North Sea has been a long-running cause of friction with our European neighbours. Britain is the only country bordering the North Sea to dispose of sewage sludge in this way. From 1980 to 1988, about 8 million tonnes a year of sewage sludge were dumped in waters around the UK, containing large amounts of metals such as lead (140 tonnes in 1988), cadmium (2.4 tonnes) and mercury (1 tonne). The rivers are an even more significant source of such chemicals.

# North Sea Conference objectives

The objectives set by the North Sea Conference first held in November 1987 represent a step in the right direction. The conference set up new benchmarks by which to judge Britain's environmental performance – and exposed our shameful record hitherto.

In order to combat pollution of the North Sea, those states with a direct interest gathered in November 1987 to try and formulate an action plan to protect the sea. The subsequent Agreement includes a commitment to substantial reductions, of the order of 50 per cent, of inputs to rivers and estuaries of certain especially hazardous substances: those with persistent toxicity and which build up in living tissue or are concentrated in the food chain, such as cadmium and mercury.

The Government has attempted to comply with some aspects of the Agreement. However, it still prevaricates over other aspects, such as reducing nutrient inputs to the North Sea which over-fertilise the water. For instance, the Government denies that our input of nutrients such as nitrate to the North Sea has helped to cause the devastating algal blooms that have occurred. Other signatories to the North Sea agreement have called for all the surrounding countries to take action, and West Germany has proposed much greater treatment of sewage to remove nutrients (nitrate and phosphate) before the effluents are discharged.

By the time of the third North Sea Conference in 1990, Britain was under pressure to conform and get rid of the 'dirty man of Europe' epithet. In March 1990, the Secretary of State for the Environment announced an end to sludge dumping by 1998 – a rather long way off, but nevertheless a clear commitment. Waste incineration at sea is to be phased out by the end of 1990, a year ahead of the schedule. This should not distract attention from other inputs into the seas. In 1988 the UK still discharged nearly twenty tonnes of mercury, nearly sixty six tonnes of cadmium, almost one and a half tonnes of the pesticide lindane and over three hundred thousand tonnes of nitrogen into our coastal waters. These emissions via rivers and through direct discharges into the seas were a considerable improvement on what had gone before!

# Bathing beaches

Another problem, of which all too many of us have unpleasant personal experience, is the contamination of bathing beaches by raw or inadequately treated sewage.

This has long been a source of contention between the Government, the British public and the European Commission. In January 1990, and again in the White Paper on the Environment published in September 1990, the Government proudly boasted that 76 per cent of bathing water 'met European quality standards', but this statement has to be put into context. Firstly, the extremely warm, sunny weather in 1989 had helped kill off bacteria and viruses and so had increased the level of compliance with European standards. Perhaps more significantly, the Government was being economical with the truth over the actual standards being met. Subsequent analysis of the figures by Friends of the Earth showed that 49 of the bathing waters which the Government claimed had 'passed', had in fact merely passed *some* of the standards, but had failed the standards for either viruses or salmonella bacteria. Additionally, another 135 bathing waters had not been tested for compliance with these two standards and so may have failed as well. The simple fact is that British bathing water is a lot less clean than you may have been led to believe.

Currently, 87 per cent of sewage outfalls to coastal waters have virtually no treatment. This legacy of neglect provoked such an outcry amongst the public that the Government was compelled to commit the water industry to a £1.4 billion construction programme to improve the situation. Unfortunately, the programme was based upon the construction of much longer pipes for discharging the sewage, rather than better treatment. The problem was simply being pushed further out to sea. The Government's official line was that the dilution and natural disinfectant properties of seawater were enough to protect health and the environment – a claim hotly disputed by environmentalists.

Then, after an intensive campaign by Friends of the Earth, the Marine Conservation Society and others, the Secretary of State for the Environment made an astonishing U-turn. On March 5th 1990 Chris Patten announced that an extra £1.5 billion would be spent by the water industry. In general, sewage discharged to estuaries will receive additional secondary treatment (sedimentation and biological digestion). Some coastal discharges will still only receive primary treatment (separation of gross solids by sedimentation), but this will be an improvement on the mere maceration and screening that is the common sewage 'treatment' along the coast now.

This was a considerable victory for the groups that had campaigned for years for clean beaches, but more was to come. In a scathing report published on July 11th 1990, the House of Commons Environment Committee called for full biological treatment for all sewage discharges into the sea wherever possible, including nutrient removal where necessary. The report was warmly welcomed by Friends of the Earth as another step towards a cleaner healthier Britain. The Government has yet (September 1990) to publish its official response, but it is unlikely to be enthusiastic. Certainly, the Environment White Paper made no further commitments to improvement of sewage discharges.

*Friends of the Earth Policy Recommendations*

## Sea Pollution

**1.** All sea-dumping of industrial waste and sewage sludge should end as soon as technically feasible.

**2.** The Government should ensure compliance with all the requirements of the North Sea Conference Agreement.

**3.** All significant discharges of sewage effluents to the marine environment should be subject to secondary (ie biological) treatment as a minimum requirement.

**4.** All discharges of sewage effluents to marine waters sensitive to over-enrichment by nutrients should be subject to tertiary (ie nutrient removal) treatment.

**5.** The Government should ensure that all marine and freshwater bathing waters meet *all* the standards in the EC Bathing Water Directive.

# Rivers and groundwater

In 1988, the results of a nationwide survey of eels taken by the Ministry of Agriculture, Fisheries and Food from 62 UK rivers were revealed. Analysis showed high levels of poisonous chemicals such as the pesticide dieldrin and toxic PCBs. Eels caught in England contained on average three times the amount of dieldrin recommended as safe for human consumption by the Department of Health. The most contaminated eels contained ten times this level.

The Prime Minister has claimed that the Thames is the cleanest metropolitan estuary in the world, but the survey results are still far from acceptable. Below the Beckton sewage works, PCB concentrations in eels of up to 9.3 milligrams per kilogram (mg/kg) were found. At ten sites, four of them on the Thames, the eels contained mercury levels above the 0.3 mg/kg level set by two EC Directives.

All too often, river pollution finds its way into the water we drink. In 1989, the *Observer* collaborated with Friends of the Earth on a survey which showed that millions of UK consumers are supplied with drinking water which fails to meet one or more European standards. Standards breached include those for lead, aluminium, nitrate and pesticides.

Leaking waste dumps and toxic algae also threaten water supplies.

River pollution incidents have become ever more frequent. The Government's figures for 1988 showed a fifteen per cent rise on the previous year, and the total – 26,926 cases – was more than double the 1980 figure. Industry, agriculture and sewage were the chief culprits.

# River quality

Norfolk rivers are by no means alone in suffering from the effects of toxic pollution. PCBs have been detected in many other places. The River Lowman, source of drinking water for thousands of Devon households, was recently found to contain 'fish, eels and other wildlife' that were 'riddled with PCBs' in the words of *Today* (April 25th 1990).

The classification scheme for British rivers is deplorably vague. There are only five categories, ranging from 'high quality' to 'grossly polluted'. These classes are so broad that significant deterioration within a class can go unrecorded, as the Nature Conservancy Council has pointed out. The scheme makes no provision for incorporating conservation criteria for protecting freshwater wildlife habitats.

However, even the lax scheme in use cannot disguise the fact that many British rivers are of poor, and in some cases worsening, quality. Only Scotland, and on urbanised stretches of certain major rivers such as the Tyne, Tees and Mersey, has there been real improvement. Overall, the official National River Quality Surveys show an overall decline in river quality for the period 1980–85 (the most recent national survey data available). In general, the very bad rivers have got better but some of the very best rivers have got worse. There is a trend towards mediocrity in our rivers. In the south west, only 34 per cent of the rivers that were meant to be in the top category of river quality actually reached their targets in 1986.

It is to be hoped that the new National Rivers Authority (NRA) will enforce higher standards and reverse the decline. But as we shall see, there are growing fears that the Authority will not be given the resources to carry out this vital task. If it is not, our rivers will continue to lack the protection they deserve.

# The pollutants 1: Nitrate

Because of the acknowledged risk to public health, both the EC and the World Health Organization (WHO) set limits for nitrate concentrations in public water supplies.

Government figures show that some 1.6 million people were supplied with water that failed to meet the EC limit (50 milligrams per litre) at some time in 1987. The worst-affected areas were in East Anglia, Lincolnshire, Notting-hamshire and Staffordshire.

Behind this widespread contamination lies the general intensification of British agriculture and the massive increase in agricultural fertiliser applications. These rose from an average annual figure of some 60,000 tonnes in the 1940s to a total in 1985 of around 1,600,000 tonnes. Annual losses of nitrogen through leaching into both ground and surface water stand typically at around 70 kilograms per hectare per year, but in intensively farmed areas, losses more than twice as high are possible.

Leaching through soil into underground water supplies can take up to twenty years. This is a long-term problem, and the worst may well be yet to come. A long-term solution, which must involve a cutback in fertiliser applications, is imperative.

Action is being taken – belatedly. It has taken persistent EC pressure, culminating in the threat of prosecution (following a formal complaint by Friends of the Earth), to shake the Government's complacency. Even now, reliance is placed on the notorious voluntary approach. The Government has set up ten 'Nitrate Sensitive Areas' (NSAs), covering 37,000 acres, in a pilot scheme. Farmers will be paid to farm in ways that are less likely to cause nitrate pollution – in other words they will be paid not to pollute our drinking water. The National Rivers Authority has described the NSA scheme as 'an insufficiently secure base on which to proceed.'

Furthermore, there are already signs that some farmers in the NSAs will not participate, significantly weakening the scheme's effectiveness. It should also be remembered that the Government agreed to the EEC drinking water standards as long ago as 1980. It has taken them ten years just to launch a pilot scheme to control nitrate pollution at source.

# The pollutants 2: Pesticides and chlorinated solvents

All too often, unsafe practices or old-fashioned processes in industry or agriculture lead to water pollution. Dangerous chemicals cannot be permanently dumped. Out of sight, out of mind – but in the long run, they can turn up in our water supplies.

Chlorinated solvents are a case in point. One example is trichloroethylene, used for cleaning metal in light engineering industries. It is potentially carcinogenic. Such solvents regularly contaminate groundwater. In Birmingham, solvents were found in 78 per cent of boreholes examined. Fortunately, the people of Birmingham have their tap water piped in from Wales. In nearby Coventry, however, special solvent stripping equipment has been installed to clean up the affected drinking water.

Pesticide contamination is even more widespread. We will touch on this problem in our discussion of Agriculture. It is worth emphasising again that the long-term solution (as with excessive nitrate use) must lie in changing agricultural practices and in tighter controls over the use of these chemicals, including bans. For the present, investigations by the British Geological Survey and by Friends of the Earth have highlighted the growing problem.

In 1987, the British Geological Survey reported that even if pesticides were used in the approved ways, pesticides might build up in water supplies to levels above EC limits. 1987 also saw the conclusion of a major two-year survey undertaken by Friends of the Earth, which analysed data supplied by water authorities and companies and showed that there were widespread breaches of the legal limits set for pesticides, involving 298 water sources or supplies.

Active ingredients implicated in breaches of the single-pesticide limit included two chemicals, atrazine and simazine, commonly used as 'total weedkillers' by local councils and by British Rail.

Little comfort should be drawn from the fact that breaches of the pesticide standard had been recorded (as of 1987) in only six regions, all in England (Anglian, North West, Severn-Trent, Thames, Wessex and Yorkshire). It is all too probable that water suppliers in other areas had simply not carried out comprehensive checks. Tests for pesticides are difficult and expensive to carry out. This has resulted in a lack of information about seasonal variations in levels, and a general paucity of reliable data.

The Government has now advised that all water suppliers should monitor for atrazine and simazine. A survey of London drinking water carried out by the Institution of Environmental Health Officers in 1990 found that no less than 59 per cent of tap water samples contained atrazine, and 34 percent contained simazine, at levels above the legal limit.

The Secretary of State for the Environment has granted the water companies many exemptions from meeting the requirements of the legal standards for drinking water. For instance, an undertaking has been accepted from Thames Water that effectively allows them to supply drinking water with an excess of pesticides until the year 2000. Friends of the Earth is challenging this in court and has asked for a judicial review of the Secretary of State's decision.

As we shall see, pesticides in drinking water represent yet another area of environmental concern in which the British Government has tried to hold out against European standards.

# The pollutants 3: Lead and aluminium

Lead enters drinking water from old service pipes owned

by water suppliers, and from the plumbing in many older buildings, including hospitals and schools as well as private houses. It can impair the mental development of small children and may threaten unborn children as well since it can cross the placental barrier from the mother's blood to that of the foetus.

Lead is a particular problem in Scotland and the north of England where there is a large amount of lead piping and soft water which dissolves lead. Having sought to defer meeting the EC lead limits in 1985, the Government admitted some two years later that they were still widely breached in Scotland. A programme to treat water chemically so that it absorbs less lead has begun, but it is taking too long to produce the necessary results. In March 1989, no less than 70 Scottish supplies – out of the 103 originally identified as exceeding European limits – had yet to comply with the standard.

Later that year, in December 1989, Government experts reported that the present UK standard for lead (50 micrograms per litre) was not tight enough to provide adequate protection for either adults or children. Similarly, in the USA, the Environmental Protection Agency has proposed a far more stringent limit for lead in drinking water – only 10 micrograms per litre. Friends of the Earth are demanding that the lead standard should be tightened, but the Government has so far failed to act, despite the advice of its own experts.

Nevertheless, the Government used the Environment White Paper as an opportunity to laud its efforts and promised, to 'reduce human exposure to lead wherever practicable'. If this is sincerely meant, then the Government should tighten the standard for lead in drinking water without further delay, and help fund an extensive programme of lead pipe replacement.

Aluminium, possibly linked with Alzheimer's disease, is widely used by water suppliers in treatment processes. The

Friends of the Earth water quality survey identified some 150 English and Welsh districts where aluminium concentrations breached the European limit of 200 micrograms per litre. In the worst case, levels were four times greater than those legally permitted.

# Toxic algae

Press reports in the spring and early summer of 1990 drew attention to a worrying increase in the number of inland waters affected by algal blooms. Sewage, farm pollution and the phosphates in many washing powders cause nutrient pollution which allows algae to thrive, covering the water with an unattractive – and sometimes unhealthy – scum. In one of the worst affected regions, water supplied by Anglian Water Services to some 1 million people may have been affected (*Sunday Times*, April 29th 1990).

There is controversy about the possible effects on human health. Research carried out by Professor Ian Falconer at the University of New England, Australia, points to a possible cancer threat from microcystin, a toxin produced by a species of blue-green algae. Professor Wayne Carmichael, a US expert, was reported in the *Sunday Times* as believing that the toxin might cause nausea, diarrhoea and skin rashes.

The danger to health may be unproven, but there is obviously cause for grave concern. Uncertainty still prevails over the dangers of algal toxins getting into tap water, but the National Rivers Authority has warned anglers and water sports enthusiasts of the possible risks due to toxic algal blooms in lakes and reservoirs.

The water companies may well have cause to regret the laxity of pollution control in the past, especially if warmer summers lead to mounting problems. 'A good summer,' as the *Observer* put it (May 6th 1990), 'could cause an unprecedented toxic algae crisis.' Dozens of reservoirs may face closure just at the time when water supplies are at a premium. Friends of the Earth, commenting on the report published by Anglian Water Services into the 1989 incidents, said: 'The water industry has tried to close its mind to a problem that has been staring it in the face.'

Not until January 1990 did the public have the legal right to see full analyses of the contents of their tap water. A clause in the Water Act 1989 now allows a consumer to visit a register of water quality or request a written copy – free of charge – from the water supplier. However, access to data for areas other than the customer's own supply zone is still restricted by cost. Under the Water Act 1989, water companies may make a 'reasonable charge' for such information.

# Sewage

Sewage disposal provides a telling illustration of the Government's willingness to compromise environmental protection in the face of pressure from private companies.

The serious flaws in the present set-up have been outlined in two recent authoritative reports. The House of Commons Environment Committee produced a report in 1987 which showed that pollution from sewage works had been rising through the 1980s – and which was highly critical of official policy. The Committee stated that 'we are convinced that improvement to sewage works' effluent is necessary in order to arrest the recent small net decline in water quality and to secure long-term improvement in river quality overall.'

The 1987/8 report of Her Majesty's Inspectorate of Pollution (HMIP) stated that a fifth of water authority sewage works were in breach of the law in 1987, as they had been the previous year. The Inspectors blamed antiquated equipment and poor maintenance. They called for increased capital investment 'to replace aging unsatisfactory plants . . . In some cases it would be necessary to reverse the trend towards unmanned works.'

Although the 1989 Water Act repealed the general duty laid on the Government to maintain and improve the quality of rivers, Whitehall had by now acknowledged the need for 'urgent improvements'. In late 1988, water authorities had been instructed to upgrade substandard sewage works 'in the shortest practicable timescale' – about three years.

Far from being a trailblazing environmental initiative, this was yet one more belated shift of position under growing expert pressure. The plain fact is that the Government itself must bear much of the responsibility for the underlying drop in standards. Control over sewage works is exercised through 'discharge consents', which specify how polluting the effluent is allowed to be and lay down standards for specific pollutants such as ammonia. Far from tightening up this key regulatory mechanism, the Government had been deliberately relaxing the consent standards.

During the 1980s, discharge consents were relaxed for 1,800 of the 6,600 sewage works then in operation. Had this not been done, the water authorities might have faced prosecution from members of the public under the 1974 Control of Pollution Act. Then in 1989, the Government relaxed the consents for nearly 1,000 more works in order to avoid the embarrassment of selling off the water industry with sewage treatment works which broke the law. Again, had this not been done, the companies involved could have faced prosecution – scarcely an attractive prospect for potential investors.

It is worth pointing out that this original relaxation of standards was an 'alternative' – a poor one, to be sure – to the investment in new plant which water authorities were prevented from making by the Government itself. Rigid

Whitehall-imposed financial constraints encouraged, and virtually forced, water authorities to neglect maintenance and forego modernisation. The entire sewage and pollution control system was undermined. Water authorities more or less gave up any attempt to properly enforce standards: 26,926 water pollution incidents were reported in 1986, but only 327 prosecutions resulted.

In a letter to a supporter of Friends of the Earth (June 2nd 1989), the Government claimed that there was 'no question' of its allowing 'a reduction in water quality and pollution control standards'. To put it bluntly, this claim contradicts the facts. Relaxing discharge consents amounts, precisely, to a reduction in pollution control standards.

# Agricultural pollution

We have already highlighted the threat posed by nitrate fertilisers and pesticides leaching from agricultural land into rivers and groundwater. Alongside this long-term problem, there has been a steep rise in one-off farm pollution incidents. Spills of silage effluent and slurry are a particular worry. Slurry is one hundred times as polluting as raw human sewage, whilst silage effluent is two hundred times as polluting. The effects of spills on rivers can be devastating, de-oxygenating the water and wiping out fish on the affected stretches. One incident in the Anglian region in 1989 killed over 10,000 fish and affected 60 kilometres of the River Black Bourne in Suffolk, when 3 million gallons of pig slurry breached a retaining earth bank.

Farm pollution incidents are generally on the increase. There was a 267 per cent rise from 1979 to 1988, when a record total of 4,141 cases were reported. Last year saw a fall in the number of incidents, but this was mostly due to dry weather rather than any improvement in pollution control.

29

The increase in farm pollution followed a period of Government inaction. In its 1985 Waste report, the Royal Commission on Environmental Protection (RCEP) had recommended tighter controls over grant-aided farm waste disposal systems. The recommendation was rejected: indeed, Government spending on grants for farm waste management was actually cut in July 1986. Only in 1988 did the Ministry of Agriculture make available £50 million, over a three year period, to rectify the situation. The delay over such a relatively small sum graphically illustrates the short-sighted and penny-pinching attitude of the Government.

It is also disturbing that the Secretary of State for the Environment has not yet acted under the 1989 Water Act to allow the National Rivers Authority to prohibit or restrict polluting practices in designated water protection zones. As we have seen, the time-honoured 'voluntary approach' was preferred in the case of nitrate applications. Even though farmers can no longer defend themselves against pollution charges by pleading 'good agricultural practice', the present system amounts to locking the stable door after the horse has bolted. Tougher powers of enforcement are needed.

The Government has now proposed draft regulations which will set standards for the construction of silage clamps and slurry lagoons. However, these will only apply in the first instance to new or enlarged installations, whilst it is the old ones that are the problem. The proposals received a further airing in the Environment White Paper, but the Government failed to mention there that the implementation is already several months late. As in so many cases these controls will be meaningless without proper enforcement – and yet the NRA is hopelessly understaffed. In the south west region there are nineteen pollution field officers for 20,000 dairy farms.

# The 'Red List'

The Government's July 1988 consultation paper on controlling water discharges of particularly dangerous substances was a significant development. The proposals cover a 'Red List' of 23 chemicals (including cadmium, mercury and the pesticide dieldrin) which have been identified as priority substances for control.

This constitutes a significant shift in Government policy, away from setting discharge standards according to the potential for dispersal or assimilation in the water, and towards an acceptance of the need to control emissions at source by 'best available technology not entailing excessive cost'. This approach will help the UK to meet the obligations it accepted at the North Sea Conference in 1987 to reduce the amounts of the most dangerous chemicals entering the North Sea. The Government has been forced to begin to abandon its earlier reliance on the Environmental Quality Standard (EQS) approach, which was based not on actual emissions but on their dispersal and assimilation in the water.

# EC pressure: nitrate and pesticides

Over nitrate and pesticides, too, British Government inaction has been exposed by pressure from our European partners. As we have seen, the problems in both fields are acute. The Government's failure to comply with EC Directives makes a mockery of its claims of environmental virtue.

In 1986, Friends of the Earth complained formally to the European Commission over the UK Government's failure to comply with the Drinking Water Directive. Faced with the threat of legal proceedings, the Government acknow-ledged that it was breaking the law in two respects. First of all, it had advised water suppliers that the EC limit of 50 milligrams per litre for nitrate in drinking water could be regarded as a three-month average figure. In fact, the limit is an absolute one, not to be exceeded in any single sample. In the second place, it had granted exemptions under the Directive ('derogations', as they are known) on the basis that the nitrate pollution problem was due to the nature and structure of the ground. This is not the cause of nitrate pollution.

Following this forced admission of its own illegal con-duct, the Government withdrew the derogations it had granted to no less than 48 water supplies.

Equally scandalous have been the British Government's attempts to evade EC standards for pesticides in drinking water, which came into force as long ago as July 1985. Far from taking action to bring drinking water into line with the standards, the UK has been pressing the European Com-mission to propose to modify the Drinking Water Direc-tive, replacing the current pesticide standards with others, in most cases laxer.

In the meantime, water suppliers are, in effect, being encouraged to break the law. Under the circumstances, the Government hardly qualifies as the 'competent authority' entrusted with enforcing the European quality standards.

# The National Rivers Authority

The National Rivers Authority (NRA) is one of the few pollution control initiatives taken by the Department of the Environment to regulate the newly-privatised water industry. Here again, EC pressure was decisive: under the original privatisation plans, the industry was to have been responsible for controlling its own pollution (judge and jury, gamekeeper and poacher, all in one). The EC warned Britain that an independent 'competent authority' was required. Legal opinion taken by the Council for the Protection of Rural England enforced the same view.

Thus the Government was forced to set up the NRA. Nevertheless, the NRA is potentially a most important step forward in pollution control in the UK. Potentially – but only if it is adequately funded, adequately staffed and given sufficient powers. So far, the signs are not auspicious.

The NRA was originally referred to as 'the strongest environmental protection agency in Europe' by its government-appointed chairman, Lord Crickhowell, at its beginning in 1989. By the time of the White Paper on the Environment a year later, the Government had diluted this boast to 'one of the strongest environmental protection agencies'. The NRA estimates a total shortfall in Government grant-in-aid of nearly £105 million by 1994.

In the summer of 1990, the Authority made urgent representations to the Government. According to the *Sunday Times* (April 15th 1990), in submissions to the Department of the Environment, the NRA argued that it 'is so short of staff, equipment and money that many rivers will stay filthy and polluted unless the Government makes more resources available.' Lord Crickhowell stated that unless more money was forthcoming, the Authority 'wouldn't be able to pursue monitoring, supervision and cleaning up as quickly as we would like'.

The NRA also suffers from the limits of the extent of its powers. So far, it has not been given powers of legal prohibition or restriction in water protection zones. The 1990 Environmental Protection Act has also weakened it by handing its control over discharges of 'Red List' chemicals to Her Majesty's Inspectorate of Pollution. Friends of the Earth commented: 'The NRA doesn't seem to have any political clout. It is not only losing in the field but also in the corridors of power.'

For Britain's groundwater, rivers, lakes, estuaries and coastal waters, the lack of a well-funded and powerful watchdog could be a disaster.

*Friends of the Earth Policy Recommendations*

# Water Pollution

The Government should implement the following recommendations, which supplement those in the sections on Agriculture and Hazardous Wastes.

**1.** Water protection zones should be designated in sensitive water catchments, to provide tighter control over land use and to control pollution from diffuse sources (such as pesticide usage) that affects water quality. [*Partly reiterated as 'Pesticides' Policy Recommendation #11*]

**2.** The Government should ensure that all drinking water, including that from private supplies, complies with the legal limits set in the EC Drinking Water Directive.

**3.** The 1989 Water Act should be fully implemented.

**4.** Discharge consents for sewage treatment works should be tightened where appropriate, and sufficient capital funding should be provided to modernise and maintain all ageing and/or overloaded treatment plants.

**5.** In water catchment areas especially sensitive to

pollution, and/or where drinking water sources are already polluted, pesticide use should be strictly controlled – and banned if necessary.

**6.** The 'polluter pays' principle should be enforced. Where drinking water sources are polluted with pesticides and associated 'inert' ingredients and breakdown products, water suppliers should install the best available treatment technology to minimise contamination and prevent toxic by-products forming. The manufacturers of pesticides should be made legally liable for the costs of treating drinking water to eliminate pesticide pollution.

**7.** The Government should establish and monitor strict quality controls for pesticides in the environment, based on levels needed to safeguard human and environmental health.

**8.** Statutory river quality standards should include explicit criteria for nature conservation.

## Chapter 3

# BURNING IT UP: OUR ENERGY RESOURCES

Few human activities affect the environment as much as our use of energy. As we have seen, emissions from British power stations are a major cause of acid rain. A recent report from the Government's own Energy Technology Support Unit (ETSU) at Harwell has suggested that electricity generation produces as much as 25 per cent of all Britain's global warming gases. Nuclear power – which proved too expensive and risky to privatise – is still being given Government support at a time when we are as far as ever from finding convincing solutions to the safety and radioactive waste problems that have always dogged the nuclear industry.

However, it is not just electricity generation that is a problem. UK energy use as a whole – in industry, homes, offices, cars and so on – is currently responsible for the emission of nearly 600 million tonnes of carbon dioxide ($CO_2$) a year: three per cent of the world's emissions of the most significant greenhouse gas from one per cent of the world population. Our use of natural gas causes leaks of methane, a powerful greenhouse gas, from the gas-pipe network, and Britain has not avoided the marine and coastal devastation which can be caused by oil pipeline leaks and tanker disasters.

Energy, then, is a key area for environmental action – and for Government initiatives.

The present level of Government thinking is illustrated by the comment of former Energy Secretary Cecil Parkinson, who assured Friends of the Earth that his objective was to ensure 'adequate secure and environmentally acceptable supplies of energy in the forms that people want and at the lowest practicable costs.'

This is a hollow claim, even in its own terms, as it flies in the face of Government policies both before and since the statement. More disturbingly, it reveals the basic truth that this Government is unwilling to consider the heart of the matter in energy politics: no one wants energy.

What people want is the services which using energy can provide – warmth in winter, cooked food and cold beer, manufactured tools to make work easier, travel . . . When politicians talk of 'demand for energy' as an excuse for building more power stations or opening new oil pipelines, they forget that the demand is not for the electricity or the oil, but for the things we can do with these when we use them in various bits of hardware – buildings, appliances, boilers, motors, light bulbs and so on. The demand is for energy services.

How much energy is needed to meet this demand depends, very largely, on the design and performance of the end-use hardware. Improving the energy efficiency of the hardware can provide the same or better service for less energy input. That means less impact on the environment.

Light bulbs are one example. A 'normal' incandescent 60 watt (60W) light bulb uses 60 watts of electricity to produce its light output. When this light bulb is used, there needs to be 60 watts of power station output ready to come on stream.

However, there are bulbs – known as 'compact fluorescents' or 'low energy light bulbs' – which are far more energy efficient and can produce as much light as a normal

37

60W light bulb for just ten watts. Instead of having 60W of power on stream, just ten watts are needed. The same lighting output is produced for just one-sixth of the pollution! Over the lifetime of the bulb, the output of as much as one tonne of carbon dioxide could be saved, as well as cutting other pollutants.

It follows that government policies need to concentrate at least as much on the 'demand side' – on the energy efficiency of the hardware – as on the 'supply side' – what type of power station or fuel we use. In Britain, the Government has barely had an energy *supply* policy. It certainly has no energy demand policy.

Above all, a clear government commitment to energy efficiency is needed. In February 1989, Friends of the Earth's evidence to the House of Lords Sub-Committee on Energy, Transport and Technology concluded that widespread application of state-of-the-art energy efficient technologies could cut average UK electricity demand by at least 70 per cent, from 28 gigawatts (28 thousand million watts) to 8 gigawatts. Peak demand could fall from about 50 to below 15 gigawatts. Reports from the Energy Technology Support Unit have shown that major savings are also technically possible and cost-effective for other 'non-electric' energy uses.

Investing now in energy efficiency improvements can satisfy the demand for energy services every bit as effectively as building new power stations. It costs far less, sometimes between five and ten times less, and its environmental impact would be far lower.

Now is the time, too, for a clear shift of research funding towards the development of safe, cleaner alternative energy sources.

But no lead is coming from the Government. The newly privatised electricity companies have been rigged to push for increased demand, so they can keep their profits up. And while 'renewables' are starved of funds and given demanding financial targets, the risky and economically profligate nuclear industry is being shored up.

# Energy efficiency

In 1985 the British Government was party to an EEC commitment on energy efficiency which called on Member States to reduce, by 20 per cent by 1995, the amount of energy needed to produce £1,000 of economic output. This is more or less the rate of improvement which Britain achieved between 1979 and 1989. It is not at all clear, however, that the improvement has had anything to do with Government policies to improve energy efficiency. In 1987 the Paris-based International Energy Agency (IEA) estimated that it was very largely due to the decline of Britain's heavy, energy-intensive industry over the decade. A large proportion of every £1,000 of economic output is now due to the work of service industries than due to traditional industries like steel making. Insurance workers can produce £1000 of economic output with a lot less energy than can a steel-worker! The IEA reported that little of the improvement was due to energy efficiency improvements themselves.

Of more significance for the environment is that in 1989 the UK consumed as much energy as it did in 1980. Given the vast potential for energy efficiency improvements, this fact is an indictment of the Government's lack of will.

# What can be achieved

The technologies are available. Countries such as Sweden have introduced tight regulations which set high standards for insulation and efficiency of building: triple or even quadruple glazing is standard on Swedish houses. In

Britain not even double glazing is needed to meet the latest building regulations.

In 1987, in the United States, President Reagan signed into law the National Appliance Energy Conservation Act which sets legal minimum energy efficiency standards for a range of domestic appliances such as fridges and freezers. This Act is tough enough to ultimately outlaw between 70 and 90 per cent of the models on sale in the shops in 1986. According to the American Council for an Energy Efficient Economy, the Act will save the output of 21 large power stations and the annual emission of 70 million tonnes of $CO_2$ by the year 2000.

Friends of the Earth has calculated that if a similar proportion of the inefficient appliances on sale in the UK was outlawed, we would save 10 million tonnes of $CO_2$ every year by early next century. This represents 10 per cent of emissions due to domestic electricity use. If standards were tightened towards the best available technology in Europe we would save as much as 25 million tonnes of $CO_2$ a year. As Friends of the Earth puts it: 'By preventing the sale of inefficient models, we can give people a real opportunity to "buy energy efficient" and to help reduce pollution.' Yet the Government has refused even to introduce a legal requirement for all appliances on sale to be labelled to show how energy efficient they are.

The White Paper, *This Common Inheritance*, indicates that the Government has now accepted that both labels and standards are necessary. However, the Government is still pushing for a voluntary approach even though its own reports indicate that legislation is probably required to ensure compliance.

There is scope for greater efficiency in electricity generation through combined heat and power (CHP) schemes. CHP stations can be very small-scale, costing less than £50,000 to buy and install. They use fuel up to twice as efficiently as conventional coal-fired stations. Conventional stations waste some 60 per cent of the heat they produce by putting steam into the atmosphere via their giant cooling-towers. In CHP schemes much of this waste heat is recaptured and used for heating local homes, offices and industrial processes. Many homes in West Germany and Denmark are heated this way.

The Energy Technology Support Unit has advocated much greater use of CHP generators by large energy consumers in Britain, such as hospitals, hotels and leisure centres. They would sell surplus power to the grid or buy in extra power as needed. Government experts estimate that such small CHP stations could meet as much as 10 per cent of UK electricity demand, with resulting cuts in emissions of 4 per cent for carbon dioxide and 12 per cent for sulphur dioxide.

Greater flexibility for small stations to feed into the electricity grid is one of the few plusses of the Government's electricity privatisation (see below). If greater CHP generation results, that will be a small but welcome contribution to energy efficiency.

As we have noted, building design is another area where much greater energy efficiency is possible. A recent feature in the *Independent on Sunday* (April 22$^{nd}$ 1990) highlighted the energy saving achieved by London architect Stephen Reyburn in his three-bedroom house in Hammersmith. The house is superinsulated: the six-inch wall cavities (two inches is the usual gap) are filled with mineral fibre; there are ten inches – double the norm – of roof insulation; and the building materials, triple-glazed windows and carefully thought out solar aspect all contribute to energy saving. Ventilation is via a heat exchanger which warms incoming air with heat extracted from the old air being expelled.

The result? Anticipated heat loss is up to ten times lower than in a conventional house. Mr Reyburn is not installing solar heating yet, because he doubts that he will need it: 'If I can virtually heat the house off a light bulb, putting in solar heating may be gilding the lily.'

41

This is just one example – and admittedly, it is state-of-the-art. However, the Energy Park housing estate at Milton Keynes has shown that similar methods can be applied on a large scale. One key to ensuring that they are applied lies in setting much higher efficiency standards for the building industry. The new set of building regulations the Department of the Environment brought in on April 1st 1990 fell far short of what is required. Friends of the Earth described them as 'approximately at the standard Sweden was at in the 1930s'.

Both consumers and the environment would soon feel the benefit if stringent standards were set. Super-insulation of new homes often costs little more than standard building techniques and can pay for itself in lower heating bills within less than five years. For most older existing homes, draughtproofing, cavity wall and loft insulation and better central heating controls will also pay for themselves in less than five years and can save up to 50 per cent of fuel use.

'The Government should bite the bullet,' Professor Peter F. Smith, chairman of the Royal Institute of British Architects, told the *Independent on Sunday*, 'and raise insulation standards to Scandinavian levels.'

# The Energy Efficiency Office

As well as setting tough standards for new building, the Government should be promoting energy efficiency research and encouraging consumers to save energy. This is the job of the Energy Efficiency Office.

Government protestations about the need to conserve energy have to be treated sceptically in the light of the fact that the Energy Efficiency Office's budget has been cut repeatedly. From £22.5 million in 1986/7, it fell to £15 million in 1988/9, and the projected 1990/1 figure remains at £15 million in spite of all the Government's fine words about the value of energy efficiency. It is hardly surprising that Michael Colvin MP, a member of the House of Commons Committee on Energy, remarked in May 1990 that 'the Energy Efficiency Office does not seem to do much'. Resources, and morale have been relentlessly sapped.

The Government's entire record since 1979 on energy conservation has been patchy – and worsening. Peter Walker's 'Monergy' campaign of 1986–87 perhaps deserves credit for raising public awareness, though its 'Monergy' message was somewhat obtuse – save energy, save money, save 'monergy'! But that campaign has not been followed up. On the contrary: in June 1988, the Government decided to stop grants assisting industrial consumers to undertake professional energy surveys. At the same time, the loft insulation grants programme was cut back by almost a third. And for a good measure, the TV advertising campaign promoting household energy saving was also halted.

When in 1989 the Department of Energy moved into its swish new offices near Buckingham Palace, the Energy Efficiency Office was stuck out in a draughty old office block awaiting the property developer's bulldozer – out on a limb both politically and literally.

The process of revitalising the Energy Efficiency Office may have begun with the White Paper; several new 'initiatives' (mainly an expansion of current activities) have been announced for the Office. However, no new money was forthcoming, indicating that the Office's scant resources will be spread even more thinly.

Against this background of cutbacks and complacency, how can the Government claim to be playing a leading role in facing up to the threat of global warming?

# Electricity Privatisation

Department of Energy civil servants working on electricity privatisation got the choice of offices in the new building. No annexe for them. The privatisation has dominated the Government's energy policy thinking since the 1987 election. It followed the privatisation of British Gas which made the company's profits dependent on constantly increasing gas sales.

For the Government, the great nuclear power fiasco was the most embarrassing aspect of the electricity privatisation programme. Environmentally, the worst aspect is the fact that commercial logic, in the absence of appropriate regulatory constraints, will simply encourage the privatised utilities to sell as much electricity as possible.

Moreover, the 1989 Electricity Act missed the opportunity of guaranteeing a sizeable market for renewable energy.

Altogether, electricity privatisation is bad news for the environment. It need not have been, but the choices which the Government made in designing the structure and regulation of the privatised industry condemn both the industry and the environment to a more fragile future.

# The incentive to consume

The local Electricity Boards now have every incentive to sell more power, rather than promoting energy conservation. If the Boards fail to increase sales then their profits will suffer badly. Yet every extra unit of electricity sold will lead to nearly an extra kilogram of $CO_2$ entering the atmosphere.

A particularly disturbing and absurd illustration of the free market logic now governing electricity supply was revealed in a recent article in the *Independent* (April 15th

1990). The newly privatised companies are offering discounts, ranging from 10 to 25 per cent, to large-scale users. Those with consumption exceeding the one megawatt mark benefit from these discounted prices.

As many as 1,000 electricity consumers are 'borderline cases'. They now have an incentive to maximise their consumption, to keep above the threshold – and save money. The Association for the Conservation of Energy has calculated that the efforts of these users, mostly factories and hyperstores, to get on the right side of the borderline could generate as much as one million tonnes of carbon dioxide annually.

Similar incentives encourage gas users to exceed the 25,000 therm per year threshold, and here too the result will be increased greenhouse gas emissions. A school near Peterborough was reported by BBC Radio's *File on Four* to be heating its rooms to over 80°F in the hot May of 1990 in order to use enough gas to qualify for the cheaper rate, thus saving several thousand pounds.

If the right regulatory and pricing framework is put in place, privatised electricity supply need not lead to profligate consumption. In New England in the USA, the electricity company is investing some $200 million over the next few years helping people install energy efficient equipment and insulation in their homes and offices. Because of the regulatory framework governing the local electricity company there, this power saving will prove to be a far more profitable route to follow than building new power stations to produce extra power.

In the UK, however, no appropriate measures have been taken. It is not as if the Government did not have its chance. While the Electricity Act was passing through the House of Commons, the Government rejected all amendments promoting energy efficiency. The House of Lords amended it instead, incorporating a strong legal commitment to energy efficiency. Yet the Government was prepared to accept only a watered down version of the Lords' amendment, merely giving the Office of Electricity Regulation powers to set standards in the promotion of energy efficiency. This regulatory body can merely tell the Area Boards to hand out leaflets on energy conservation, set up a telephone advice line, and so on.

The Boards still cannot do what their counterparts in the USA can do – make more money out of energy efficiency investments than out of energy supply investments. Indeed, the terms of the regulations mean that electricity companies will not even be able to recoup the costs of energy efficiency improvement works by passing them on to their customers in the way they can the costs of new power stations.

It is imperative that the Government changes the regulatory framework. Investment in energy efficiency must be treated on the same basis as investment in new or replacement power plants. Distribution and generating utilities must be allowed to recoup efficiency investments through charges.

# Nuclear versus renewables

A UK Government delegation to the Intergovernmental Panel on Climate Change advocated 'economic pricing of energy alternatives to promote development of energy alternatives and energy efficiency.' We have just seen how energy efficiency is faring under privatisation. Alternative energy based on 'renewables' is unlikely to do any better.

The electricity distribution companies will be obliged to buy a massive 20 per cent of electricity from nuclear sources, but only a paltry 1,000 mega watts – less than 2 per cent – has to come from renewables by the year 2000. Moreover, renewables will have to earn rates of return on capital of around 12 to 15 per cent, while nuclear power, which the Government was unable to privatise, will only have to satisfy public sector norms (currently 8 per cent returns).

Far from redressing the historic imbalance between nuclear and renewable energy, the Electricity Act could make things worse.

# Nuclear Power: 'Too cheap to meter'?

In 1979, the Thatcher Government, newly elected, announced its intention of building ten pressurised water reactors (PWRs) by 1990. Ten years later, after the City's refusal to 'buy nuclear', it has ended up going ahead with just one, Sizewell B – an expensive face-saving exercise. Sizewell B apart, there is a five-year moratorium on new nuclear stations.

Environmentally, the nuclear industry has never been acceptable. The collapse of the Government's ten PWR programme has to be good news for the Planet. However, there are disturbing signs that the Government would like to keep the nuclear option open despite the strong case against it.

At the Sizewell B inquiry between 1983 and 1985, the Central Electricity Generating Board (CEGB) claimed that nuclear power was cheaper than coal. Now, the electricity industry is admitting what Friends of the Earth has been arguing since 1973: far from being cheap, nuclear electricity costs far more than the coal-fired alternative – as much as twice the price. According to a report in the *Sunday Correspondent* (April 8th 1990), CEGB chairman Lord Marshall, who had become known as 'Mr PWR' because of his unfailing commitment to the technology, was advising ministers in 1987 that the long-term cost uncertainties of nuclear power would make it unattractive to investors.

The House of Commons Energy Committee's report on electricity privatisation was reaching the same conclusion in 1988: 'We are worried about the cost of nuclear power . . . We are certainly persuaded that many of the critical assumptions which underlay the inquiry inspector's view that Sizewell B will be economic are no longer tenable.'

The Government had been warned. Indeed, similar and even stronger reservations had been expressed by another Select Committee as long ago as 1981: 'Enormous past nuclear investments have had exceptionally low productivity: great resources have been used with little direct return and a serious net loss.'

Sizewell B looks set to repeat the problems. According to secret documents leaked to Friends of the Earth in June 1990, the costs of construction are spiralling and could run to £3.8 billion. This is to produce electricity which Friends of the Earth has calculated will cost as much as £1 million per day more than power from a gas-fired station. One year's worth of that, £365 million, could buy the country enough low energy light bulbs to save more electricity than Sizewell B would ever produce. The day after Friends of the Earth leaked the documents, and editorial in *The Times* called for the immediate cancellation of Sizewell B.

## Radioactive contamination and radiation monitoring

The Government's response to the Chernobyl disaster in April 1986 revealed official ineptitude and poor communications with the public and between government departments.

The whole event, we were told, would be over in a few days (though not for the citizens of the Soviet Union, many hundreds of thousands of whom have suffered evacuation, become ill or died). Four years after the accident, and over

2,000 miles away, more than half a million sheep in Britain were still affected.

In the spring of 1990, North Wales hill farmer Trebor Roberts told the *Guardian* (April 27th 1990) that he still had to ask permission from the Ministry of Agriculture, Fisheries and Food every time he wanted to move sheep down from the high pastures. Up there, where rainfall is heaviest, radioactive caesium-137 levels are still continuing to rise as contamination moves from moss and lichen into grass, from where it is more easily taken up by sheep.

'Now,' says Trebor Roberts, 'someone from the Ministry has told me quietly he thinks the land could be contaminated forever.'

The Government's Chernobyl monitoring exercise altogether missed a number of 'hot spots' such as Skipton Moor in Yorkshire, surveyed by the Friends of the Earth Radiation Monitoring Unit.

It should be noted that in March 1989, a CEGB paper to the Institute of Mechanical Engineers showed that a Chernobyl-like reactor core melt-down could happen in Britain's older 'magnox' nuclear power stations. Such worst case scenarios now form part of the safety design assessments – the unthinkable is being thought.

Monitoring of contamination from home-produced British radionuclides has been just as lax as for Chernobyl fall-out. The Ministry of Agriculture, Fisheries and Food fails to check all the likely exposure pathways. Two recent cases, both involving radiation from Sellafield, have been pinpointed by Friends of the Earth. In December 1988, an area of contaminated land was found next to the River Esk, in Cumbria. In April 1990, more contamination, also from Sellafield, was detected along the Rivers Lune and Wyre, which are 60 km from the Sellafield discharge pipe. On these rivers, as much as 22 km up river, contamination four times higher than recommended limits and sixteen times higher than the investigation limits was found.

## Radioactive waste

The Government has no coherent policy for radioactive waste management. Just before the 1987 General Election, it withdrew the proposal to build a low-level waste dump at one of four prospective sites: Fulbeck, Elstow, Bradwell and South Killingholme. All four sites are in Conservative Parliamentary constituencies. In all four places, there had been unanimous and vociferous local opposition to the plans.

In November 1988, the Department of the Environment published figures on the amounts of radioactive waste awaiting disposal: 517 cubic metres of high level waste, 59,400 cubic metres of intermediate level waste, 2,300 cubic metres of low level waste.

NIREX, the industry's civil nuclear waste disposal company, is keen on burying the waste deep underground. However, a study jointly commissioned by Friends of the Earth and Greenpeace in March 1989 – 'Exposing the Faults' – showed that it is simply not possible to be certain about the safety of waste stored in a deep repository for the thousands of years needed for it to become safe. The day before the study was launched NIREX announced that they had chosen two 'geologically suitable sites' to investigate for a dump – one at Sellafield, and the other at Dounreay in Scotland, both owned by the nuclear industry.

Sellafield was an apposite choice. As the centre for reprocessing the spent fuel from nuclear reactors – a process believed by many in the industry to be totally unnecessary – Sellafield is Britain's principal source of radioactive waste by volume.

In April 1990, a team of six scientists from the International Atomic Energy Agency (IAEA) confirmed the Friends of the Earth and Greenpeace criticisms of NIREX's deep disposal plans. The IAEA's anxieties included the danger that rock formations would prove unstable (or would be destabilised by storage operations), allowing radiation to escape; the possible effects of chemicals in the waste on concrete containment barriers; the corrosiveness of salt water likely to be found in the proposed locations; and the still unsolved problem of how to let possible gas build-ups escape while keeping radiation sealed in.

Also in April 1990, Friends of the Earth published a survey of thirteen countries which showed that Britain alone had no timetable laid down for dealing with its radioactive waste problems. The survey, conducted by an independent geologist, was critical of NIREX's failure to carry out adequate research into the suitability of the relevant rock formations.

Meanwhile, the Government continues to hold open the option of dumping waste from decommissioned power stations in the sea, a policy reiterated in the White Paper.

At the same time, British Nuclear Fuels Plc, the owner and operator of Sellafield, continues to sign lucrative deals to process nuclear waste from overseas. Much of the contaminated material will remain here. A massive £225 million deal with the West German nuclear industry will keep the new Sellafield reprocessing plant (known as THORP) busy for ten years. This follows the German Federal Government's decision to shelve plans for a reprocessing plant at Wackersdorf, because German environmental rules made the project uneconomic (and also, perhaps, because of intense public opposition to the project). Part of the proposed site at Wackersdorf is now to be used for a factory making solar heating panels.

Here in Britain, it seems, we are less careful and less mindful of the future – and nuclear waste goes on accumulating.

**Personal radiation exposure limits**

UK legal limits for personal exposure to ionising radiation were set in 1985. The Government is reluctant to update them. For workers in the industry, the annual limit is 50 milliSieverts (mSv). For the general public it is 5 mSv.

In 1987, following an intense campaign by Friends of the Earth involving more than 800 international experts, major reductions in these limits were recommended by the Government's own advisory body, the National Radiological Protection Board (NRPB). The dose for industry workers should be cut to 15 mSv, said NRPB, and a new site-specific limit should regulate the dose members of the public can receive from any one site.

The proposed new site limit of 0.5 mSv is ten times lower than the current blanket limit for the general public. Up to 2,000 workers in the nuclear industry are currently thought to be exposed to annual doses exceeding the new NRPB recommendation. However, the Government is taking no action to enforce the new guidelines.

In February 1990, the Gardner report, published in the British Medical Journal, showed that the children of workers exposed to doses lower than permitted levels were still at significant risk of developing leukaemia. The risks indicated a need to get dose limits down by a factor of five immediately.

Friends of the Earth commented:

> The study shows that radiation is considerably more dangerous than thought when the current safety standards were set. The Government has consistently put the needs of the nuclear industry before the need to protect the health of its workers and their children.

### The future of the nuclear industry

Following the electricity privatisation debacle – the reversal of the decision to sell off the nuclear power stations – the Government stated that no new nuclear power stations would be built before 1994. However, it is clear that the Government wants to keep the nuclear option open. It claims it is worth spending the money on Sizewell B because we nay need nuclear power to help curb global warming. Yet the Friends of the Earth study, *Getting Out of the Greenhouse*, shows that nuclear power is one of the most expensive means of cutting emissions of carbon dioxide (the main greenhouse gas) and that massive cuts in UK carbon dioxide emissions are possible with measures cheaper than nuclear power.

The requirement that the new electricity supply companies purchase nuclear power, the disadvantaging of renewables in terms of financial targets, and the very unequal allocation of research funds all make plain the Government's determination to protect the nuclear industry – despite its poor economic record and its manifest environmental dangers.

# Research and renewable energy

Given the fact that fossil fuel power stations produce greenhouse gases and are a major cause of acid rain, and given the economic and environmental failings of nuclear power, future energy sources must comprise a large and growing reliance on renewables such as wind, wave and solar power. The Department of Energy now admits that by 2025, 30 per cent of UK electricity demand could potentially be met through renewables.

If this target is to be met, renewable energy must operate in a favourable financial regime. Moreover, research into renewable energy must be a priority. Unfortunately, neither condition is being met by current government policy.

We have seen that whereas nuclear power is set relaxed public sector financial targets and given a guaranteed large market share, renewables receive no such grand favours. A report in the *Mail on Sunday* (April 1st 1990) indicated that the European Commission had set down financial constraints that will militate against renewable energy.

The British Government appeared reluctantly to accept the Commission's ruling, which limits the period of subsidy for renewable and alternative energy to the end of 1998. Subsequent research by Friends of the Earth has shown that the European Commission was doing what the Department of Energy in Britain had requested.

More than 300 schemes, involving wind, tidal power and the combustion of waste gases from landfill sites, are threatened. Originally, their promoters were told that the projects would receive subsidy for between twelve and fifteen years. Now, the Commission's ruling risks making the schemes largely unworkable.

Friends of the Earth stated: 'We cannot afford to lose the environmental benefits of such valuable technologies.'

Equally unsatisfactory is the past and present pattern of research funding.

Nuclear fusion is almost certainly science fiction – or science fantasy. It has no record of success and there is no reason to believe it will ever be economic. But fusion research is still receiving £25 million a year – with few questions asked about viability, completion dates or cost-effectiveness.

Fast breeder research is another high-tech folly with little application to the real world. Admittedly, the Government has begun to cut funding. In future it plans to put its effort into European research. However, the House of Commons Energy Committee reported in July 1990 that, with £4 billion spent over 35 years of research at Dounreay, no further work could easily be justified, either in the UK or in Europe.

Overall nuclear research and development is still costing Britain more than £200 million a year. Money channelled through the UK Atomic Energy Authority alone totals more than £16.3 billion since 1958. Half of this has come directly from Government and is equivalent to a hidden subsidy of 1.25p per kilowatt hour for every unit of nuclear electricity ever generated.

And renewables? Total research expenditure has been less than £200 million since 1975. Currently, just over £20 million is spent annually on renewable energy research and development. This remains a quite inadequate investment in what should be a central element of our long-term energy strategy.

# Gas, oil and coal

Natural gas, oil and coal remain central to current energy supply (indeed, nuclear power and hydro-power meet less than seven per cent of UK energy demand). In the long term, these fossil-fuels must be supplemented and eventually largely replaced by far less polluting alternatives. If we continue to burn them at the current rates, the environmental implications are awesome. However, this does not remove the need for prudent management at the moment. Wise management of these valuable resources has not been the hallmark of Government policy.

### North Sea oil

The Government's stated strategy for North Sea oil is to go for 'maximum economic exploitation'. In practice, this means getting the oil out of the ground as fast as possible, and then selling it regardless of the price it fetches.

In 1988, the UK produced 44 per cent more oil than it consumed. However, if extraction continues at these rates the days of the UK oil surplus are numbered. Production levels will soon start falling and will diminish inexorably until resources are depleted – possibly well before the middle of the next century. Yet we use far more oil than we need to meet the UK demand for energy services, particularly in the ever-profligate road transport sector.

Quite irresponsibly, the Government seems prepared to sanction environmental destruction for the sake of a marginal prolongation of oil supply. A particularly glaring instance was the Department of the Environment's decision to allow offshore drilling at Poole Harbour as an extension to the Wytch Farm oil field complex. This amounted to a statement that the whole country was up for grabs. As the Chief Planning Officer for Dorset said:

> If oil development is allowed in an area which is a Site of Special Scientific Interest, an Area of Outstanding Natural Beauty and part of a Heritage Coast, there are few locations where it could legitimately be refused.

## Coal

Since 1984, productivity in British Coal mines has risen by 65 per cent. Nonetheless, there is a shift away from deep coal mining and a reduction in overall output. Open cast mining is increasingly favoured by British Coal because it is far less labour intensive and therefore considered cheaper. Yet open-cast coal has a higher sulphur content than average British deep mined coal and therefore produces more emissions which help cause acid rain.

In addition, as the Council for the Protection of Rural England points out, up to 2,500 hectares of countryside are being irreparably damaged each year, with excavation depths of up to 200 metres.

There is also a move, actively encouraged by Government, towards importing low-sulphur coal from abroad. This is then used to reduce the amount of flue gas desulphurisation (FGD) equipment needed in order to meet EEC targets for cleaning up acid emissions. This may save money for the power generation companies, but it merely exports the environmental damage wrought by open-cast mining to other parts of the world, like Colombia and Australia.

These policies are extremely short-sighted. Once a mine is closed, safety dictates that it should be 'sterilised': flooded to prevent fires (water pollution from abandoned mines is a widespread problem in Britain), or deliberately collapsed. It is then very costly to reopen the mine in question. Today, our theoretical reserves of coal are being radically reduced. Britain, it used to be said, has coal enough to last for a good 300 years. As a direct consequence of current policies, based on short-term market considerations, potential reserves could fall to as low as fifty years. This may serve to severely limit our options in the foreseeable future, when coal will still have to play a part in providing energy in Britain, particularly as more efficient and far cleaner coal-combustion technologies are developed.

## Gas

The failure to address environmental problems at the time of electricity privatisation was rehearsed with the Gas Privatisation Act in 1986. British Gas profits are tied to ever-increasing sales of gas. And now, the gas industry is poised to move in to supply gas for electricity generation as private enterprise looks for power stations which are cheaper, more efficient and quicker to build than traditional coal and nuclear stations.

Gas-fired 'combined cycle' plants offer these particular advantages and the Government is encouraging their uptake by relaxing the obligations of power generating companies to fit FGD equipment. Gas-fired power stations have lower acid emissions and higher efficiencies. However, they still waste 50 per cent of the energy in the gas and a third of electricity generated in the UK is used to provide just the kind of low grade heat which gas provides so well directly. That makes it somewhat absurd to burn the gas in a power station rather than directly in a boiler in the home or factory. In addition, gas leakages from the pipe network and production system add significantly to the threat of global warming and could seriously undermine any advantage gas may have over coal in terms of 'cleaner' emissions.

## *Friends of the Earth Policy Recommendations*
## Energy

**1.** The Government should introduce measures to encourage energy conservation and efficiency, to result in an annual reduction of national energy consumption of at least one per cent per year, starting now. This will require major improvements in building standards, legally binding minimum efficiency standards for appliances and a comprehensive scheme for the mandatory labelling of all energy-consuming goods.

Through grants and tax incentives (for instance linking mortgage tax relief to the energy efficiency of the home), the Government should promote the widest possible use of state-of-the-art, energy-efficient technologies. It should take particular care to use them in its own buildings. [*Reiterated as 'Global Warming' Policy Recommendation #1, partly as 'Eco-labelling' Policy Recommendation #2*]

**2.** The Energy Efficiency Office should be expanded to coordinate a national energy efficiency programme, including Combined Heat and Power schemes and district heating schemes. [*Reiterated as 'Global Warming' Policy Recommendation #2*]

**3.** The Government should restructure the electricity and gas industries into energy service industries in which energy efficiency investments are profitable.

58

*[Reiterated as 'Global Warming' Policy Recommendation #3]*

**4.** The Government should establish a Renewable Energy Development Agency to promote the use of energy from renewable sources and the development of a domestic renewable energy industry.

**5.** The Government should immediately make a five-fold reduction in dose limits for radiation exposures, and review justification procedures for worker exposure.

**6.** The Government should immediately abandon the construction of Sizewell B PWR nuclear station and remove all state support for nuclear power.

**7.** All radioactive discharges from the Sellafield reprocessing plant should cease.

*Chapter 4*

# OUR FARMS AND FORESTS

1989 was Food and Farming Year – an unfortunate choice as it turned out. First salmonella and then listeria hit the headlines. Since then, public anxiety about just what goes on down at the farm has been heightened by the outbreak of bovine spongiform encephalopathy (BSE), popularly known as 'mad cow disease'. US official documents have cast new doubts on the safety of the bovine somatotropin (BST) milk-boosting hormone, which British Agriculture Minister John Gummer approved for experimental use, while refusing to disclose the location of herds to which it is being administered. In late 1989, dairy and beef farmers in southwest England were banned from marketing their produce when their cattle ate imported feed contaminated with lead.

As well as raising doubts about the healthiness of some of the food produced, intensive farming practices damage the long-term fertility of the soil. In 1988, the Soil Survey of England and Wales revealed that no less than 44 per cent of arable land was at risk from soil erosion.

Nitrogen run-off from intensively cultivated and ferti-lised farmland increases nitrate levels in drinking water sources (see the section on Water Pollution) and helps spark off 'blooms' of algae in inland and coastal waters. The Norfolk Broads, internationally important for wildlife, 'now rate as one of the most contaminated wetlands in the world', according to Dr Rosalind Boar, lecturer in environmental studies at the University of East Anglia. Agricultural pollution of the water catchment area feeding the Broads is believed to be one of the major causes.

So far, Government attempts to redress the balance have proved ineffectual. The Ministry of Agriculture, Fisheries and Food (MAFF) has a statutory duty to promote not just production, but recreation and conservation too – a duty imposed in the 1986 Agriculture Act – but this aspect has received low priority. MAFF seems unable to represent consumers in their anxiety about food quality and animal welfare and does little to promote sustainable agriculture (agriculture compatible with the long-term health of the soil and the wider environment). While small farmers continue to go out of business and the environmental viability of extensive chemical-based farming grows ever more questionable, MAFF clings to outdated notions.

We need a Ministry that will conserve the countryside, promote consumer demands for safe and unadulterated food, *and* defend the real interests of the rural economy. Applying the principles outlined in the Brundtland Report (*Our Common Future*, Oxford, 1987), and adopting the Policy Recommendations we give below, would be steps in the right direction. Existing piecemeal legislation is simply not enough.

# Food: BSE, BST and battery farming

Bovine spongiform encephalopathy (BSE) is a fatal disease of the nervous system in cattle. Until three years ago, it was unknown. To date its occurrence has only been confirmed in British cattle (and in one case in Ireland and in cattle in Oman imported from Britain). As of the summer of 1990, cases were being diagnosed at the rate of some 250 per week, and 20,000 cattle altogether had contracted the disease. This figure was originally estimated to be the final toll reached in 1993, when the disease was due to have run its course. A similar illness, involving 'spongy brains' and nervous system disruption, has been observed in domestic pets and zoo animals. A condition in humans known as Creutzfeld Jakob disease shows similarities with BSE, too, but no connection has been proven.

The cause of BSE is thought to be the transmission of a disease through the unnatural practice of feeding cattle, which are vegetarian, cud-chewing animals, the remains of other animals as protein feed. The official working party on BSE chaired by Sir Richard Southwood, the Southwood Committee, acknowledged this when it reported that 'in every case of BSE investigated so far, animal protein had been fed to the animal.' The feed concentrates given to affected cows included the ground-up remains of sheep. The practice of using offal for animal feed has now been banned following the development of BSE in a pig experimentally injected with infected cow brain.

It is hardly surprising that many consumers now wonder whether it is safe to eat beef. In July 1990, the all-party House of Commons Agriculture Committee concluded that the measures enacted 'should reassure people that eating beef is safe'. However, the official working party had sounded more cautious, stating:

The potential routes of transmission of BSE from cattle to humans have been examined closely. With the very long incubation period of spongiform encephalopathies in humans, it may be a decade or more before complete reassurance can be given.

It is clear that the Government was slow to respond when the disease began to appear. Initially, compensation for suspect animals was paid at only 50 per cent of their value, and there can be little doubt that, as a result, affected cattle entered the food chain. Compensation has now been raised to 100 per cent.

Moreover, BSE is a symptom of the wider malaise of intensive livestock rearing. It is an indictment of practices that, quite apart from the inhumane treatment of animals which they involve, fail to produce truly 'cheap' food. Both for farmers and for consumers, the outbreak of BSE has been a reminder of just how dangerous, and how costly, current practices can prove.

There may well be problems, too, in the administration to milking herds of the yield-boosting synthesised animal hormone bovine somatotropin (BST). Drug comanies are keen to foist BST on farmers and consumers. This makes sense in terms of pharmaceutical industry profits, but it has nothing to do with need, animal or human.

BST is a genetically engineered hormone capable of boosting milk production by 20 per cent. However, Britain and the EEC are awash with milk and dairy products already. The European Community has some 120,000 tonnes of butter in intervention storage. Against that background it is not surprising that the European Parliamentary Committee on the Environment, Public Health and Consumer Protection concluded that there was 'no justification for the strategic use of BST or for that matter any product which could increase milk production still further'.

What of the potential health risks? Agriculture Minister John Gummer went on record with the view that there was 'no justification for not authorising BST on scientific grounds'. However, evidence from the US Food and Drug Administration points to a wide range of abnormalities suffered by cows injected with BST. These have included enlarged organs and udder infections. Moreover, abnormally high levels of the hormone were found in the cows' milk.

One might have thought that consumers would at any rate be given the choice as to whether they drank BST-treated milk or not. Since 1986, however, ten experimental herds in the UK received BST, and milk from them has entered the market, where it is not distinguished from milk from untreated herds. Because of their designation as 'experimental', the British herds were not covered by the European Commission's moratorium (due to expire at the end of 1990) on the use of BST.

As well as making a nonsense of attempts to curb the over-production of milk, BST also undermines legislation passed in 1986 which outlawed animal growth-promoting hormones. Since it boosts growth of calves as well as milk yields, its misuse offers a relatively easy way for unscrupulous farmers to evade the ban.

The battery hen system has been criticised for years, but successive governments have been unwilling to reform or abolish it. Some 25 years ago the Government-appointed Brambell Committee advocated better treatment of animals reared for human consumption. Dr Thorpe, a member of the Committee, subsequently wrote to *The Times* (June 23rd 1968) to complain that MAFF had taken no notice of its recommendations, bowing instead to 'pressure from people in the battery business'. Dr Thorpe reminded readers that the Committee had concluded that 'there was no justification for keeping animals in greater densities than the absolute maximum we laid down.' But industry profits were given precedence over expert advice.

In 1981, the House of Commons Agriculture Committee recommended that battery systems be banned within five years. At present, hens are still incarcerated three to a cage, with each bird enjoying less space than the area of a sheet of A4 paper.

Switzerland is to outlaw battery farming from 1992. In the Netherlands, many poultry are reared in systems which allow them to follow their natural behaviour patterns. Swedish animal protection law states as a fundamental principle that 'the technique should be adapted to the animal' rather than vice versa.

If and when free range poultry rearing is widely introduced in the UK, that will highlight the need for an adequate standard definition of 'free range'. At present, some free range flocks are thousands strong, preventing the establishment of a pecking order: as a result, birds actually rarely venture outside the building. A maximum density of some 150 birds per acre would be an appropriate criterion for a tighter definition of 'free range'.

# Farming and conservation

Despite the ending of capital grants for hedgerow removal and drainage of wetlands, wildlife habitats are still being damaged or destroyed as a result of intensive farming practices. In 1989 alone, 228 Sites of Special Scientific Interest (SSSIs), key wildlife sites whose importance is officially recognised, were damaged. Agriculture, accounting for some 92 cases, was the single greatest culprit. In the first half of the 1980s, hedgerows were being lost at the rate of 4,000 miles a year: unfortunately no more recent evidence exists as to whether the rate of destruction slowed down, speeded up or remained constant during the later 1980s.

The Government has recently announced, in the White Paper on the Environment, its intention to give local authorities the power to protect hedgerows of 'key importance'.

Agricultural policies still give priority to production, at the expense of careful management of the countryside. The

1986 Agriculture Act, as we have noted, did contain a welcome acknowledgement that food production must be balanced with other considerations. The Act recognised the need to achieve a 'reasonable balance' between four considerations:

a) the promotion and maintenance of a stable and efficient agricultural industry;

b) the economic and social interests of rural areas;

c) the conservation and enhancement of the natural beauty and amenity of the countryside (including its flora and fauna and geological and physiographical features) and of any features of archaeological interest there; and

d) the promotion of the enjoyment of the countryside by the public.

However, the means proposed for the pursuit of the Act's conservation objectives are inadequate. Environmentally Sensitive Areas (ESAs), environmental 'top-up' payments for farmers opting for 'set-aside' schemes, and the Farm Woodlands Scheme (discussed in our review of Forestry, below) all represent welcome new thinking. However, they involve only a small proportion of farmland, and receive only a tiny fraction of the public money devoted to maintaining and boosting agricultural production. Additionally, they are all voluntary schemes.

It is worth observing that this emphasis on production has not just been at the expense of the countryside. Many farmers and farmworkers have lost out as well. Since the Second World War, farmers have decreased in numbers at the rate of some 4,000 a year, with small farmers in particular disappearing. From a figure of some 450,000 farmers on the land in 1945, the total has dropped to 225,000. The National Economic Development Office foresees this figure eventually falling, if present trends continue, to as low as 90,000 – just one farmer for every two current members of Friends of the Earth!

As farmers have got fewer, farms have got bigger.

Typically the sale of a farm means its amalgamation with another farm. Farmworkers' jobs are lost and farm accommodation is sold off for non-agricultural residential use. This trend is evidenced by the fact that in Britain, just eleven per cent of all farmers are now responsible for 57 per cent of food production. Rationalisation can also involve wildlife habitats being damaged.

# Environmentally Sensitive Areas

The introduction of designated Environmentally Sensitive Areas (ESAs) in 1986 has been perhaps this Government's single most important initiative to encourage a better balance between farming and conservation. The scheme encourages farmers 'to adopt special agricultural management practices aimed at protecting and enhancing the environment.' Local features such as stone walls and wildlife are protected and maintained. While it is true that *all* farming should be 'environmentally sensitive', ESAs are a small step in the right direction because they establish the principle and practice of paying farmers for doing something for the environment other than producing food.

However, because of inadequate funding, the scale and impact of the ESA initiative remains very small. Initially, 310 potential ESAs were put forward, reduced to a shortlist of 46. To date, only nineteen have actually been designated. The scheme is voluntary, and of the 790,000 hectares that fall within the ESA boundaries, agreements have only been concluded in respect of 235,000 hectares. This represents just 1.3 per cent of agricultural land in Britain.

The current total budget for the ESAs is £12.6 million. In contrast, £1.3 billion was spent in 1989 in the UK on intervention in the market, price regulation, and other production-related items. The ESA scheme is 25 per cent funded by the EEC. In future, money saved by reducing guarantee payments to farmers for price support should be redirected into schemes such as ESAs, enabling the extension of 'environmentally sensitive' farming to the whole country.

# Set-aside

Although it was accompanied by considerable publicity, the set-aside scheme has achieved almost nothing in environmental terms. Two hundred and sixty thousand hectares were meant to have been 'set-aside' by the end of 1989, but in the event the figure was a mere 110,000 hectares. As with ESAs, the scheme is voluntary, and the area covered hitherto represents just 2.8 per cent of the total cereal area, or 0.6 per cent of all agricultural land in the UK. Set-aside is not targeted to either sensitive water catchment areas, or land vulnerable to erosion.

The real intention of the measure was to reduce cereal surpluses. It is not working. The EEC grain harvest for 1990 is estimated to be some 170 million tonnes, while the maximum level set by the EEC, above which price cuts for next year's harvest will come into force, is 159 million tonnes. Further technological advances in crop breeding and biotechnology, together with the fact that the yield-boosting capacity of nitrogen fertiliser is not yet exhausted, mean that set-aside cannot possibly deal with the problems of excess grain production in the EEC.

By paying farmers to take up to one fifth of their land out of production, the Government hopes to encourage smaller harvests. No benefit to consumers is envisaged, since prices will be held at existing levels.

There is nothing to prevent farmers being paid public money to take out their least productive land and then work the remainder as hard or harder than before, thus nullifying the hoped-for reduction in yields. This is called 'slippage' and is well-documented in the USA, where the set-aside concept originated.

The main factor limiting plant growth and crop yields is the availability of nitrogen. Nitrogen fertilisers are effectively 'land in a bag'. Production would be far more effectively curbed if nitrogen quotas, applicable across the country, were introduced. Such quotas would not only reduce production, they would also cut nitrate pollution of water sources and rivers which harms the aquatic environment and contaminates drinking water. Nitrogen quotas would also be much fairer than radical price cuts as a means of cutting production. Price cuts would squeeze farmers' profit margins, encouraging them to attempt to force even more out of the land to survive economically. The end result of savage price cuts would almost certainly be the loss of even more small-scale farms.

Top-up payments for additional environmental management introduced to set-aside farmland have been introduced by the Countryside Commission as a 'pilot scheme' in seven areas. These are an attempt to 'bolt on' environmental benefits to a scheme which originally lacked any convincing environmental rationale. Moreover, the five-year initial time-scale of the set-aside scheme is too short to allow wildlife to become securely established in new habitats. If there is to be an effective 'set-aside' policy then strips of land should be left uncultivated along the margins of rivers and streams to protect water from agricultural pollution, which, along with strips running beside hedgerows and field margins, would provide vital 'wildlife corridors'.

Set-aside could also have a role in protecting sensitive water catchment areas. In some parts of the country, this may mean that certain types of farming will not be viable. All rivers, streams and lakes need to be protected from agricultural pollution. The right strategy to control surpluses is to introduce quotas and to encourage more extensive farming practices throughout the country linked to ESA payments.

# Soil erosion

As we noted above, almost half (44 per cent) of arable land in England and Wales has been classified by the Soil Survey as at risk from soil erosion. The Soil Survey, which monitors this serious problem, has recently suffered cuts in its budget. The situation is particularly serious in areas such as Norfolk and West Sussex: in some places annual topsoil losses through erosion have been recorded as high as 200 tonnes per hectare.

The underlying cause is that the price support system has encouraged the ploughing of former grazing land, which is essentially unsuited to arable farming. The Sussex Downs are a case in point. The crop losses resulting from erosion may not become apparent for many years, and even for generations, since they are masked by yield gains from the application of agrochemicals and from the use of new high-yielding crop breeds. In the long term, however, such farming is not sustainable.

More direct and immediate costs are borne by local authorities and communities whose drainage systems are silted up by soil run-off from eroded fields. Flooding at Rottingdean in East Sussex has caused damage and necessitated remedial work costing £1 million.

Soil erosion itself was not even mentioned in the Environment White Paper. The Government declared its continued firm commitment to 'supporting efficient and productive farming', which indicates that the agricultural norm will continue to be intensive, even though the methods used may not allow sustainable agriculture in the long term in many cases.

# Organic farming

Consumer demand for organically grown food is increasing. The Government has declared its support for organic farming, but does very little to promote it materially. The 1989 budget for what might loosely be called 'organic research and development' was £400,000 out of a total UK agricultural research budget of £200 million. It should, however, be noted on the credit side that in 1987 the Government set up the United Kingdom Register of Organic Food Standards (UKROFS), and that a survey of one thousand organic farms is to be initiated. However, much of the research and development has been left to small underfunded charitable organisations such as the Soil Association and Elm Farm Research Centre. It has been left to Safeway and the Scottish Agricultural Colleges to set up an entire farm devoted to experimental organic growing.

This lack of Government initiative means that MAFF is poorly placed to offer expert advice to farmers interested in 'going organic', an option that attracts increasing numbers as shoppers show they are willing to pay extra for organically grown produce. At present, 70 per cent of organic produce bought in Britain is imported from overseas.

# Forestry

The Government's record on forestry issues has been decidedly mixed. Where forestry interests have clashed with conservation, conservation has often come a poor second. In October 1987, the Government rejected most of the key recommendations made by the Nature Conservancy Council (NCC) in its report *Nature Conservation and Afforestation in Britain* – recommendations designed to bring environmental considerations into new forest development and to protect important wildlife sites.

In a particularly disturbing development, the Government has recently overridden the objections of conservation groups and given the green light to further conifer afforestation in the Flow Country, an area of peatland in Caithness and Sutherland which the International Mire Conservation Group, has called 'the largest and finest example of a landscape which is thousands of years old', equal in importance and uniqueness to the Amazon or the Serengeti.

# The Forestry Commission

The Forestry Commission, as well as being responsible for tree-planting, oversees forestry policy in the UK. This sometimes puts it in a position not unlike that of the old water authorities, who both monitored river quality and discharged effluents from sewage treatment works into the rivers. Conflict between its regulatory and entrepreneurial roles perhaps explains why the Forestry Commission has been slow to acknowledge that 63 per cent of trees in the UK are in poor health, and why it still denies that this is a result of air pollution. To acknowledge the problem might well discourage further tree-planting: there is little point in planting trees if one knows they will end up unhealthy.

Similarly, the Forestry Commission has been reluctant to acknowledge that confiers planted too close to rivers, lakes and streams may well have contributed to acidification of water. It cannot claim an impartial position in making such judgements when it has been responsible for planting or encouraging others to plant conifers in unsuitable areas in the first place.

The Forestry Commission's annual planting target of 33,000 hectares makes large scale conifer afforestation inevitable. This target was confirmed in the White Paper, where it was referred to as 'traditional planting'. This may

72

sound like dappled sunlight falling through mature oaks while woodpeckers swoop from tree to tree, but in many cases means the dark, dank, industrial efficiency of the straight rows of conifer plantations. In 1988, then Environmental Secretary of State, Nicholas Ridley, announced that there should be a presumption against the planting of conifers in upland England. However, his statement made no mention of Wales and Scotland, where 90 per cent of planting takes place.

The economic and strategic value of the Forestry Commission's operations was called into question in a report produced by the National Audit Office in 1986. The report noted that 40 per cent of the Commission's reserve of planting land was 'poorer and less suitable land in the North of Scotland', and that returns on investment on such areas would probably be as low as 1.25 per cent. The conclusion was drawn that 'for a significant proportion of the Commission's planting and restocking programme', non-monetary benefits would be 'unlikely to be of sufficient value to compensate for . . . low financial returns'.

The National Audit Office also contested the claim that the Forestry Commission is a major job creator: between 1972 and 1988, the number of people employed by the Commission actually fell from 6,144 to 3,850.

Finally, the report questioned the benefits of new planting in terms of 'balance of payments or strategic considerations'. It concluded that 'no significant economic benefits' would derive from the new planting even if account were taken of those considerations.

# Woodland Grants and Farm Woodlands

In the March 1988 budget, commercial woodlands were

removed from income and corporations tax provisions. This closed the tax-dodge loophole by which rich celebrities had been able to sink their income tax into tree-planting on some of our internationally important wetland wildlife sites. The move was welcome reward for an effective joint campaign led by the Council for the Protection of Rural England, the Royal Society for the Protection of Birds and Friends of the Earth Scotland.

Shortly after the Budget, the Forestry Commission announced a new Woodland Grant Scheme, superseding both the Forestry Grant Scheme and the Broadleaf Woodland Grant Scheme. Grants for broadleaf planting increased to £975 per hectare for areas of ten hectares and over. For conifers the grant remained smaller, but at £615 per hectare (for areas of ten hectares or over) it was a massive 256 per cent more than the previously available grant.

Some 60 per cent of the cost of establishing conifer forests (about £1,000 per hectare) is thus covered by public subsidy, and the level of the grant remains the same, however big the plantation. The extra support available for broadleaf planting is very unlikely to prove enough to reverse the trend which saw 28,000 hectares of conifers planted in 1987/8, compared with just 2,000 hectares of broadleaves.

Nor is this trend likely to be much affected by the Farm Woodlands Scheme, also introduced in 1988. This is intended to encourage broadleaf planting (in particular native species such as beeches, ashes or oaks), but like so many of the Government's environmental initiatives it is purely voluntary and has been taken up on a very small scale. The target for the scheme's first three years was 36,000 hectares, but with one year to go applications had been put in for less than 10,000 hectares of planting.

Another familiar weakness of the Farm Woodlands Scheme is that it fails to target appropriate land. Whereas, if it is intended to reduce surpluses of certain intensively farmed crops, it should be targeted at these areas as part of a wider extensification strategy, under its present terms farmers can plant up their least productive land. These areas often provide very good wildlife habitats which tree planting may damage or destroy.

# The Flow Country

The Caithness and Sutherland Flow Country derives its name from the strange, swirling pattern of its pools and vegetation. Its unique landscape is home to a rich diversity of birds: greenshank, dunlin, plovers and black-throated divers all breed there in significant numbers (indeed it is home to 70 per cent of all the dunlin in the UK, and to all the black-throated divers in Europe). Its conservation value is inestimable, and it is subject to the EC Birds Directive and to the Ramsar Convention, the international convention on wetland sites. Environmentalists have put it forward as a 'World Heritage Site' and (as we have noted) the International Mire Conservation Group has recognised its global importance. Hitherto, however, the Government has refused to list it under the World Heritage Convention.

The Nature Conservancy Council had hoped that the Scottish Office would agree to draw up and implement a management plan for the Flow Country (on the lines of those implemented under the scheme for Environmentally Sensitive Areas). This would have supported local occupants and industries – crofting, stalking, game-fishing – while protecting the site's conservation value. However the Scottish Office declined to pursue this path and obliged the Nature Conservancy Council to apply for designation as a Site of Special Scientific Interest, even though the Council took the view that such a designation was not appropriate for so large an area.

Of the Flow Country's 400,000 hectares, 50,000 are now

a SSSI. A rather larger area, 60,000 hectares, is already afforested, blanketed over with alien plantation conifers, mostly planted as a tax evasion measure by wealthy, usually English, clients of forestry companies. The Nature Conservancy Council estimates that a fifth of the Flow Country's waders have been displaced and their habitats 'irreversibly damaged' by forests already planted. Nevertheless, the White Paper sought to claim that a framework agreement both allows the development of a viable forestry industry, while protecting the peatlands of Caithness and Sutherland.

In January 1989, the Scottish Office, overriding objections from the Nature Conservancy Council, approved afforestation of a further 1,400 acres of the Flow Country. The Forestry Commission has argued that another 40,000 hectares should be planted with conifers. The record of the Government and the Scottish Office hitherto hardly inspires confidence that they will resist these schemes and give the Flow Country the protection it urgently needs.

## *Friends of the Earth Policy Recommendations*
# Farms and Forests

**1.** The Government should issue a White Paper with a view to replacing the Agriculture Act of 1947 with new legislation, based on a statutory code of good agricultural practice specifically designed to ensure environmentally sensitive farming throughout the countryside.

**2.** Price support for agricultural products should be progressively reduced and public subsidy for farming redirected through structural measures and direct income aid to farmers.

**3.** In the short term, the top-up payments for the current set-aside scheme should be increased in order to encourage environmentally sensitive management; in due course, the scheme itself should be transformed into a comprehensive extensification scheme, including 'transitional grants' for farmers wishing to go organic and a programme of positive habitat management and enhancement.

**4.** The UK Government should be lobbying its EEC partners for the introduction of a non-transferable nitrogen fertiliser quota. In the meantime, Water Protection Zones should be set up, with funding for farmers as part of the extensification scheme referred to above.

**5.** The Government should introduce new regulations outlawing the inhumane treatment of farm animals, and banning the use of battery systems for poultry and livestock. Swedish animal protection legislation states: 'The technique shall be adapted to the animal and not the other way around.' The Government should adopt this ideal guideline.

**6.** The recommendations of the NCC report, *Nature Conservation and Afforestation in Britain*, should be immediately implemented as a first step towards controlling new plantings.

**7.** The peatlands of Caithness and Sutherland (the Flow Country) should be designated as a World Heritage Site under the World Heritage Convention.

**8.** Planting and management grants for broad-leaved trees should be greatly increased.

# Pesticides

In the UK alone, over £400 million a year is spent on pesticides sprayed onto farms, parks, gardens, roads, railway tracks and in homes. Another £600 million worth of pesticides were manufactured here and exported in 1988. Meanwhile, public concern about the effects on human health and the environment continues to grow.

It is almost 30 years since Rachel Carson warned of the dangers of certain pesticides in her classic book *Silent Spring*, but the Government has yet to take action on the scale that is needed.

Friends of the Earth carried out a major survey of pesticide contamination of drinking water in the period 1985–87. The results are summarised below in the section on Water Pollution. Here, let us note that 298 water sources or supplies contained levels of particular pesticides in excess of the EEC standard for drinking water.

In February 1990, the Institute of Hydrology reported that pesticide concentrations in streams draining agricultural land can far exceed EEC drinking water standards. Their work, funded by the Department of the Environment, measured the run-off of pesticides from two Ministry of Agriculture, Fisheries and Food (MAFF) experimental farms operating to 'good agricultural practice'. After a storm, they found that the concentrations of simazine and atrazine (both on the Government's Red List of especially toxic chemicals) had risen to over 200 times their previous levels in one of the streams.

# The Food and Environment Protection Act 1985

The Food and Environment Protection Act 1985 is by far

the most important Government attempt to regulate pesticide use. Pesticide approval was until 1985 controlled by a voluntary code between MAFF and the pesticide producers and suppliers. The British Government only introduced a statutory approvals system when pushed to do so by the European Commission, which was of the opinion that our voluntary registration systems were in breach of EEC free trade rules.

The Food and Environment Protection Act also included statutory powers to control pesticides and their effects on human health and the environment. These were brought into effect by the Control of Pesticide Regulations 1986 which prescribed the arrangements for the approval, sale, storage, supply, use and advertisement of pesticides.

However, while Ministers were proclaiming the need to enforce pesticide controls, cuts were actually being made in the number of Agricultural Inspectors carrying out the job! All in all, government controls have been decidedly inadequate. The modest recent increases in staff still leave the Inspectorate grossly under-resourced to monitor and enforce even these inadequate laws.

The Health and Safety Executive's most recent report on pesticide incidents, for 1989/90, showed a dramatic increase in poisonings over previous years. Over two-thirds of the incidents, including poisonings, involved members of the public. The report also showed that the majority of farm pesticide stores fail to meet government safety guidelines. These problems are hardly surprising given the inadequate policing, with less than one inspector per 75,000 hectares of agricultural land.

# Residue limits and safety testing

In August 1988, again following pressure from the EEC, residue limits for certain pesticides in particular fruit and vegetables were adopted. But the Regulations were notably weaker than had first been proposed. Limits for various pesticides used on stem and leaf vegetables, roots and tubers were dropped entirely, presumably under pressure from manufacturers and from the farming lobby. Limits for more than twenty other pesticides were relaxed.

In March 1989, the Government admitted that the approvals for more than one hundred pesticides on sale in the UK were based on safety tests undertaken in 1965 or earlier, so they had not been established as safe by today's standards. Many of these pesticides are still used, despite Friends of the Earth's call for an immediate ban. The safety review for all of them will take at least ten years. Agro-chemical manufacturers joined Friends of the Earth in calling for more resources for pesticide testing. In April 1990, the Government responded with modest resource increases but even their most optimistic timetable will fail to meet the demands of the coalition for completion of the review by 1992. In reality, it could continue well into the next century.

Friends of the Earth and Parents for Safe Food high-lighted the dangers of pesticide residues in food in February 1990. A survey of food purchased from all the major supermarkets throughout the UK showed residues of a potentially dangerous chemical called ETU (ethylene-thiourea) in common foods including tomato ketchup. ETU is derived from the class of fungicides called EBDCs (ethylene bisdithiocarbamates), the most widely used fungicides in the world. Some evidence links ETU and/or EBDC with health hazards including cancer and birth defects. The United States regulatory authorities have defined ETU as 'a probable human carcinogen' and have announced a proposal to ban the vast majority of uses of the fungicide.

In contrast, the British Government has concluded that the use of EBDC fungicide poses no risk to consumers, stating: 'The use of these fungicides on wheat and potatoes [the most common uses in the UK] does not lead to detectable residues of EBDCs or ETU in foodstuffs based on these commodities.' This claim was belied by the Friends of the Earth/Parents for Safe Food survey which revealed residues in certain potato products.

EBDC was one of the fungicides for which proposed residue limits were dropped in 1988.

This episode highlights the fact that the Government reviews of pesticide safety are all too often based on incomplete information, including inadequate pesticide residue monitoring .

# Consumer information

Friends of the Earth believes full freedom of information should apply to the results of pesticide safety tests. In the USA, the data are publicly available. Here, all test results relating to pesticides approved before October 1986 (and that means most pesticides) are officially secret. Results of tests carried out after that date are supposed to be freely available. However, despite considerable pressure, Friends of the Earth has yet to be allowed access to all the information it has requested.

The Government has also dragged its feet on food labelling. Friends of the Earth believe that if consumers are to exercise their right to make an informed choice, food treated with pesticides at any stage must be labelled. Supermarkets carry out tests, but they do not publicise the results. The Government shows little inclination to take up this proposal, despite general pressure in favour of product labelling. In the Environment White Paper, the Government made no further commitment than to examine the role for food labels to indicate production methods and crop treatments. Friends of the Earth has been pressing for the labelling of pesticide-treated food since 1984. A proposed European Commission scheme will have narrower scope, applying only to foods treated with pesticides (such as sprouting inhibitors applied to potatoes) after harvesting.

# River pollution

The Government's failure to make manufacturers liable for pesticide pollution was highlighted by a recent study carried out for the National Rivers Authority. This revealed widespread contamination of both soil and water by the organochlorine pesticide, aldrin, and its breakdown product, dieldrin, following its use on land alongside the Newlyn river, in Cornwall. Aldrin, made by Shell, is now banned in the UK but was used over many years by daffodil and potato growers in the area. The soil is so contaminated that the National Rivers Authority is considering options for cleaning the site and preventing run-off into nearby water. Farmers may have to switch to other crops or even turn the land into pasture.

Friends of the Earth are campaigning for Shell to take responsibility. The company should compensate farmers for any loss in income and clean up the site to a standard where it no longer poses a threat to the environment.

As we have noted, the Institute of Hydrology report of February 1990 and the 1985–87 survey carried out by Friends of the Earth indicate that pesticide pollution of water is a very widespread and serious problem.

*Friends of the Earth Policy Recommendations*

# Pesticides

1.  The manufacturers of pesticides should have a strict liability for their products and the consequences of their use and disposal 'from the cradle to the grave'.

2.  Applications for pesticide approvals should be placed on a public register and at least 28 days should be allowed for any person to make formal representations against the proposed approvals.

3.  Regulatory laboratories should verify the toxicological and environmental data submitted in applications for pesticide approvals. These tests should cover both the active chemicals and any other ingredients in the commercial formulations.

4.  Assessment of potential adverse effects should take account of long-term and multi-factor exposures, and effects on especially vulnerable groups and all ecosystems.

5.  Approvals should be withdrawn for any pesticide which has not been proven to be safe according to today's standards.

6.  All food treated with pesticide, before or after harvesting, should be labelled. Strict maximum residue levels should be statutory for all pesticides registered for use on food crops.

7.  No approvals should be available for any pesticide liable to contaminate water unless the applicant can provide an analytical method sufficiently sensitive to monitor compliance with any relevant water quality standard or maximum residue limit in food.

8.  There should be unrestricted public access to all

raw data concerning the toxicological properties and the results of all pesticide residue monitoring.

**9.** A 5-year programme to reduce the use of agricultural, industrial and other pesticides should be introduced, with increases in the research budget for sustainable farming systems (including organic farming).

**10.** Aerial spraying should be banned.

**11.** Water catchment areas which are particularly sensitive to pesticide pollution should be designated as Water Protection Zones within which there should be properly enforced restrictions on pesticide usage. *(Reiterated as part of 'Water Pollution' Policy Recommendation #1)*

**12.** The export of pesticides should require Prior Informed Consent from the importing country. Safety data and any regulatory restrictions would then have to be disclosed to the importer before the export process could begin.

**13.** A tax on pesticides should be levied to pay for monitoring and treatment costs and for any problems caused by pesticide use where the company cannot be charged directly or is unable to pay.

*Chapter 5*

# THE CITY
# AND THE
# COUNTRYSIDE

In the last 50 years the British countryside has come under enormous and increasing pressure. Two forces have been particularly destructive: the advance of chemical-intensive, largely monocultural farming, and the insatiable demand for development land, especially for more housing in the south. In the face of this constant 'erosion' of the country-side, the Government, far from strengthening existing protection or adopting new legislation, has sometimes seemed intent on speeding up the rate of destruction. As so often happens, Britain has resisted EEC attempts to encourage conservation. And the Government has some-times ignored the recommendations of its own scientific advisers.

## Conservation Directives
## and Conventions

Despite initial resistance, Britain is no longer opposing the

EC Directive on Fauna, Flora and Habitats (known commonly as the Habitats Directive). This is an attempt to set up a European network of wildlife habitats and could help to protect over 60 types of habitat and 1,300 endangered species. Across Europe, many plants and animals are under threat as suitable habitats disappear because of pollution, agriculture or development. The Mediterranean Monk Seal now has an estimated population of only 350, and the Loggerhead turtle of Greece and Turkey is similarly endangered. Ninety-six of Europe's 380 species of butterflies are threatened, and fifteen species are near extinction. In England, eighty-five per cent of the Dorset heathlands have been lost in the last 20 years through urban sprawl, leading to dwindling numbers of sand lizards and smooth snakes.

The Government's initial reaction to the proposed Habitats Directive was not encouraging. Speaking in November 1988, Lord Caithness, the Government spokesman on the environment in the Lords, condemned 'those who believe the country should be fit for the Brussels bureaucrats with strict regulatory methods of control', and described the proposed Directive as 'attempting to put the countryside in a glass case'.

On August 23rd 1989 the House of Lords Select Committee on the European Communities produced its report on the proposed Habitats Directive. The Committee came to a different opinion from Lord Caithness, instead welcoming 'a major Community initiative in the field of habitat and species protection'. It also stated that it was 'disturbed at the weight of evidence . . . received on the continued losses of flora and fauna throughout the Community.'

More damningly, the Commitee criticised the attitude of the Government as voiced by Lord Caithness:

The Committee regret that the United Kingdom

Government adopted an unenthusiastic approach to the first round of negotiations on this proposal in November 1988.

Discussions over the Habitats Directive continue. In particular, the 'annexes' listing the species to be protected are the cause of much wrangling. Species viewed as requiring protection in one country are hunted in another. The endangered wolf is protected in Italy, but persecuted in Spain. Additionally, the lack of funding to convert fine words into actual protection for species and their habitats is a major concern.

The Government has designated less than one fifth of the sites proposed by its own scientific advisers – the Nature Conservancy Council (NCC) – under the 1979 European Commission Birds Directive. The NCC has identified a total of 218 potential Special Protection Areas for birds, but only 40 have been designated.

Britain is also a signatory to the Ramsar Convention (agreed in 1971), an international agreement to conserve important wetlands, with particular regard to waterfowl. The UK Government signed the Convention in 1973 and ratified it in 1976. By so doing it accepted a commitment to promote both the conservation of key sites and the wise use of wetlands generally within its territory. The NCC recommended that 154 sites should be designated. The Government has only designated 44 cases.

Meanwhile important wildlife habitats are being lost. Development plans for some 80 estuaries (out of a total of 120 surveyed by the Royal Society for the Protection of Birds) currently threaten to cause serious damage to wildlife habitats through the construction of port extensions and marinas. Tidal barrages, as proposed for Cardiff Bay and the Mersey Estuary, are another threat. The Mersey Estuary is classified as a Site of Special Scientific Interest and qualifies as both as Ramsar site and a Special

Protection Area (under the EC Birds Directive). It is the third most important wintering area for ducks and waders in the UK and internationally important for migratory birds which feed on the inter-tidal mudflats.

Lord Caithness told listeners to Radio 4's *World at One* in February 1989 that the Government was 'fully committed to the conservation of our natural heritage'. But the public remained unconvinced. In August 1989, a *Daily Telegraph* poll found that 74 per cent of Conservative voters felt that the Government was not doing enough to protect the countryside.

# Catalogue of destruction

The wholesale destruction of irreplaceable wildlife habitats under the impact of modern farming and forestry was first highlighted in a 1983 Friends of the Earth report. Drawing on unpublished data from the Nature Conservancy Council, Friends of the Earth showed that since 1947, 95 per cent of wildflower-rich meadows, 80 per cent of chalk and limestone grassland and between 30 and 50 per cent of ancient woodland had been obliterated.

Many recent cases illustrate the parallel threat posed by major development plans, and show that the tide is unlikely to be turned unless Government priorities change. Secretary of State for Transport, Cecil Parkinson, approved plans to build major roads at Dover Cliffs and at Twyford Down in Hampshire. In both cases, designated Sites of Special Scientific Interest (SSSIs) will be destroyed and land within Areas of Outstanding Natural Beauty will be degraded.

Rainham Marshes in Essex is another internationally important wildlife habitat under threat from development. Entertainment giant MCA (Music Corporation of America) has joined forces with the Rank Organisation to propose a

£2.5 billion Hollywood theme park on the Marshes. If completed, this will be Britain's second biggest commercial property development ever. Much of the 1,184 acre SSSI will be destroyed: this would be the second biggest loss of SSSI land to built development since the Second World War. Rainham Marshes are larger than Wimbledon Common.

If the SSSI is developed as MCA proposes, nearly 2,000 teal will be evicted, as well as short-eared owls and hen harriers (birds of prey needing large hunting territories of the order of 100 acres or more). The developers have offered to purchase and manage wildlife sites elsewhere along the Thames Estuary. Such a 'trade-off' for planning gain would be a green light to developers, suggesting that the protection of each and every SSSI could be similarly compromised. Conservation groups are proposing an alternative development to MCA's mega-plans which would maintain the wildlife value of the site, along the lines of the internationally renowned Peter Scott Wildfowl Centre at Slimbridge in the Severn Estuary.

An additional worry is that a longstanding industrial and domestic waste disposal tip adjoins the SSSI. Some 1.5 million tonnes of toxic waste were dumped there over a twenty-year period up to 1974. In June 1990, Friends of the Earth proved that, as they had earlier suggested, the site was also contaminated with low-level radioactive waste. The development is intended to destroy over 70 per cent of the SSSI and extend onto the landfill site.

Despite the wildlife value of the site and the concerns over the adjoining waste tip, Environment Secretary Chris Patten refused to order a Public Inquiry, leaving the final decision to Havering Borough Council, who favour the theme park plan.

Conservation groups are beginning to wonder whether designation of Sites of Special Scientific Interest and Areas of Outstanding Natural Beauty has any real meaning. The

*Independent on Sunday* commented on March 18th 1990 that 'the most serious damage to the countryside is likely to carry an official seal of approval'.

No further significant proposals for protection of habitats were announced in the Government's White Paper on the Environment. Despite claiming that habitat protection is 'the key to the protection of wildlife', the Government chose to merely reiterate the current framework. Gallingly, it even claimed that most damage to SSSIs could be compensated for by expansion of the SSSI network – at best, a naive claim to those interested in the richness and diversity of the British countryside, at worst, an unjustifiable excuse for the continuing lack of effective protection for all such sites.

# Sites of Special Scientific Interest

According to Nature Conservancy Council (NCC) figures, in the period 1988–90, a total of 389 SSSIs were partially lost or damaged. Two hundred and twenty-eight SSSIs were damaged or destroyed in 254 incidents during 1989, with agriculture the most frequent cause. Only 1984/5, with 255 cases, saw a higher toll. Four SSSIs or potential SSSIs have been completely destroyed in the period 1985–88. The devastation is continuing. The Prime Minister may boast of 'great efforts to identify areas of special scientific interest because of their animal and plant life' and claim 'we have taken steps to protect them.' But the figures tell a rather different story.

Government policy for landscape and wildlife conservation is still based firmly on the 1981 Wildlife and Countryside Act. This emphasises the 'voluntary approach': farmers are compensated if they forego profits by not 'improving' the agricultural value of designated sites.

This approach is highly controversial as it is based on a

principle of paying farmers for not doing what they should not be doing anyway. The 1989 NCC annual report revealed that payments in Scotland had tripled over three years: in 1989, no less than £1.6 million was paid out there.

The most fundamental failing of the system is of course the fact that notification of an SSSI does not guarantee its protection. Three major conservation organisations – the Royal Society for the Protection of Birds, the Royal Society for Nature Conservation and the Council for the Protection of Rural England – identified twenty major development plans threatening outstanding areas of the countryside (*Independent on Sunday*, March 18th 1990). Seventeen of the sites were SSSIs. In many cases, planning permission for development had already been granted. Nicholas Ridley, then Secretary of State for the Environment, drew a distinction between those SSSIs that were 'nationally important' and those that were not. By implication, he regarded the latter group as readily expendable. It remains to be seen whether Mr Ridley's successors will make real efforts to defend SSSIs. The NCC sees them as a bare minimum if wildlife species are to be protected and habitat diversity maintained. So far, the signs are not encouraging.

Historic planning permissions are one stumbling block to protection of SSSIs. The 1981 Minerals Act gave powers to local authorities, and potentially the Nature Conservancy (now the NCC), to review and revoke old and inappropriate planning permissions. This sounds good, but in practice little has been achieved, because the 1981 Act provided for compensation. Companies like Fisons are digging up some of our best peat bogs, because they own sites with planning permissions dating back to the 1940s and 1950s. Subsequently many peatland sites have been notified as SSSIs, but the planning permission overrides SSSI status – so they're being dug up. Ninety per cent of Fisons' peatcutting operations are on land designated as an SSSI. Neither local authorities, nor the NCC, can afford the compensation necessary to 'buy off' the peat companies.

In March 1990, Joan Walley MP asked the Secretary of State '. . . on how many occasions since 1981 revocations or discontinuance orders [had] been made in respect of planning permissions granted for the extraction of peat.'

Mr Trippier replied: 'None.'

This is hardly surprising if one considers that the NCC had to pay a compensation (rumoured to be £250,000) to protect just 72 of the 2,000 hectares of the Thorne Moors SSSI in South Yorkshire. The 72 hectares are now a National Nature Reserve, but surrounding peat cutting operations are causing the site to dry out, thus threatening its conservation value.

In Lower Saxony, a major peatland area in West Germany, all existing planning permissions were revoked without compensation in 1972. Operators had to then reapply for new licences with much more stringent conditions controlling exploitation to protect the needs of wildlife, and governing after-use and site restoration.

The destructive effects of opencast extraction of minerals, notably coal and construction aggregates, are not limited to loss of habitat or landscape value. For example, the operations are noisy and often polluting, can disturb the water table, and most opencast coal has a higher sulphur content than deep-mined coal, thus contributing more to acid rain. Opencast mining has expanded as a direct result of policy changes. In 1986/7 permission was granted for opencast coal extraction on almost 5,000 hectares, compared with less than 2,000 hectares in 1983/4. Since 1987, there has been a higher rate of refusal of such applications but the provisions of the 1990 Coal Act seem likely to lead to an expansion of private sector opencast mining.

Many mineral workings are still carried out under Interim Development Orders granted in the 1940s. These can override more recent designations, as, for instance, in the Gwenlais valley in South Wales where an SSSI had been designated in 1988. There are no official figures for the number of such orders still existing, although estimates have been made suggesting that up to 60 per cent of current mineral workings may be covered by Interim Development Orders.

# The Nature Conservancy Council

The Nature Conservancy Council itself is under threat. The 1990 Environmental Protection Act split this statutory body, which has the primary responsibility for nature protection in the UK, into three separate bodies, one each for England, Scotland and Wales. Proclaimed by the Government as devolutionary, this action has been denounced as utterly crass by almost everyone else. Max Nicholson, former Director General of the NCC, wrote to *The Times* (June 19th 1990) describing the proposal as a 'disaster to environmental conservation'.

Dr Derek Ratcliffe, Chief Scientist at the NCC for 16 years until 1989, commented:

At a time when the great conservation problems are seen to be international, requiring agreed standards and coordinated action with and between nations, splitting its national conservation body is a perverse step for Britain to take. Conservation issues transcend political frontiers, and actions denying this truth damage the Government's credibility in being seen to take the environmental crisis seriously.

Many of the scientific and administrative functions of the NCC will have to be triplicated, at an estimated initial extra cost to the taxpayer of £30 to £40 million.

More importantly, the decision reflects the resentment

felt by the forestry lobby in Scotland at the NCC's commitment to its statutory duty to notify as SSSIs areas of nationally important wildlife habitat, in particular the peatlands of the Flow Country, which foresters wished to cover with conifers. Even worse, the Highland Regional Council appears to see the growing campaign to save the last of England's lowland peatbogs from destruction by extraction for horticultural peat as an opportunity to develop Scottish peatbogs for peat extraction. Such differing opinions over the value of an internationally recognised wildlife habitat emphasise the need for a UK-wide conservation strategy.

The splitting up of the NCC is particularly ironic (as Dr Ratcliffe observes) at a time when it is increasingly recognised that many environmental issues are international and interconnected, rather than bounded by national borders and interests. The proposed Habitats Directive reflects this greater awareness of the supranational importance of environmental issues. Similarly the conclusions of the Brundtland Report (*Our Common Future*, Oxford, 1987) and the evident international co-operation on global warming issues discredit limited, parochial views that any bird, plant or ecosystem is specifically Scottish, English, or Welsh.

It is already clear that over issues like the peatbogs, on which Friends of the Earth is running a major campaign, different conservation strategies may well be proposed by England, Wales and Scotland. The Government's original proposals have been modified by the appointment of a 'joint committee with an independent chairman', but it remains far from certain that there will not still be damaging differences of opinion. For instance, many birds of prey currently protected in the UK are still regarded as vermin on the large sporting estates of Scotland and Wales, as the recent deliberate poisonings of red kites in Wales reveals.

# The wider countryside: Institute for Terrestrial Ecology surveys

Surveys carried out in Britain in 1978 and 1984 by the Institute for Terrestial Ecology (ITE) have highlighted the damage done to the countryside as a whole by 'more at all costs' farming.

Over the six-year period between their surveys, the ITE concluded that 'the loss of landscape features was slowing down in East Anglia, but was probably increasing elsewhere' as a result of intensive agriculture and the spread of cereal growing. Grassland 'improvement', often involving drainage and reseeding, had led to the loss of 115,261 hectares of rough grass, 14,590 hectares of moorland, 8,754 hectares of scrub woodland, 5,836 hectares of degraded pasture and 1,459 hectares of mountain grass.

Similarly depressing results emerged when woodland was examined. Over the six years, 24,700 hectares of broadleaf woodland were grubbed up, and 11,200 hectares planted with conifers. There was new broadleaf planting: 26,000 hectares (including small areas mixed with conifers). However, as ITE noted, 'the new planting differed from the ancient woods' that had been felled. For most wildlife, the new woodlands would be no substitute at all.

The Government has gradually removed grants for the agricultural 'improvement' of semi-natural wildlife habitats, but it refuses to introduce effective controls. It has previously blocked Private Members' Bills to protect hedgerows and bring locally important hedgerows within the scope of Tree Preservation Orders. However, in one of the few novel proposals in the White Paper on the Environment, *This Common Inheritance*, the Government has finally proposed that local authorities will receive powers to protect hedgerows of key importance. Tree Preservation Orders are already available to local authorities; Friends of the Earth called for such Orders to include hedgerows in a draft Natural Heritage Bill in 1983. Nevertheless, the importance of this proposal will be partly determined by how the definition 'hedgerows of key importance' is interpreted in any legislation.

*Friends of the Earth Policy Recommendations*

## Countryside

**1.** The Government should extend the planning control system and give absolute statutory protection to all key wildlife habitats.

**2.** All sites proposed for protection under the EC Directive on the Conservation of Wild Birds 1979 and under the terms of the Convention on Wetlands of International Importance Especially as Waterfowl Habitat (the Ramsar Convention) should be protected without further delay.

**3.** Powers should be made available to local authorities to help safeguard important local landscape features on aesthetic, historical and ecological grounds.

**4.** The Government should repeal Part VII of the 1990 Environmental Protection Act, which split the Nature Conservancy Council into three separate agencies. In particular, a British-wide nature conservation body remains essential to ensure compliance with, and the success of, the EC Habitats Directive when it becomes law.

**5.** The Goverment must press for the early introduction of the EC Habitats Directive.

# Planning – the green belt

Green belts are areas around towns and cities where planning policies severely restrict development. The official aims of green belt policy are to check sprawl, safeguard the countryside, prevent neighbouring towns merging, preserve the character of historic towns and assist in urban regeneration. They were established nationally (following an initiative by the London County Council) by a Government circular in 1955, but most have only been officially approved in structure plans in recent years.

This process of definition through structure plan revision has brought the area of green belts up to 1.8 million hectares, one-tenth of the land area of England and Wales. The detailed boundaries of green belts are still being defined in local plans. Re-definition occasionally occurs in favour of development. For example, the green belt at Stone in Kent was redefined in May 1990 by the Secretary of State for the Environment to exclude a 300 acre development site for a shopping and leisure complex.

Some conservationists have long seen green belt protection as a touchstone of Government commitment to environmental protection. However, the green belt policy, in its inadequacies, in fact reflects the failure of negative planning. Development has been allowed to leap-frog over green belts, with developers preferring previously un-developed or 'greenfield' sites elsewhere, rather than making full use of derelict sites in cities.

This is not to say that green belts have no value. But without other policies they are more symbolic than effective. At all events, the Government has continued to protect them. When in 1983 the consultation draft of a Department of the Environment (DoE) circular suggested that the boundaries of green belts should be re-defined at the 'long-term' limits of development (further out from the edge of

97

urban areas), backbenchers rebelled, and the circular itself (14/84) reaffirmed the protectionist policy.

# Housing

There remains a danger that new development beyond green belts will engulf acres of greenfield sites. Housing development is the major user of greenfield sites, increasing from 3,930 hectares in 1986 to 4,370 hectares in 1988. In 1980, a DoE planning circular (9/80) stated that 'the availability of land should not be a constraint on the ability of housebuilders to meet the demand for home ownership.' This bald policy has been toned down in subsequent statements, but the bias remains in favour of builders and developers.

In recent years, housing has been a contentious planning issue, with debate fuelled by increasing concerns about affordability (relating to changes in housing policy), about town cramming (the infilling of open spaces including back-garden spaces with new housing), and about free-standing new settlements. Nicholas Ridley, as Environment Secretary, was 'minded' to overrule the result of the public inquiry into the Foxley Wood new settlement proposal in Hampshire, and to allow building to proceed despite the Inspector's conclusion that, amongst other problems, unacceptable damage would be done to a nearby Site of Special Scientific Interest. However his successor, Chris Patten, reversed Mr Ridley's policy in this case – a hopeful sign.

Nonetheless, Mr Patten refuses to rule out new settlements. There are many proposals outstanding, virtually all of which would generate significant increases in traffic and require relatively large amounts of infrastructure: sewerage, water and power supply and transport links. Since 1983 over 70 proposals for new settlements have emerged, mainly in the size range of 500–5,000 houses. The rate at which they came forward peaked in 1988, with 23 proposals that year alone. About 40 proposals were still outstanding in November 1989, in a small number of cases construction had begun, some proposals had been withdrawn and about ten had been refused permission.

The Government has attempted to deal with concerns over new settlements and town cramming by pushing local planning authorities into the firing line. Mr Patten's October 1989 statement on 'local choice' argued that the allocations of housing determined for each county by the DoE should not be questioned but that it was up to counties and districts to determine the distribution of those new homes.

Contemporary patterns of housing development are inherently environmentally damaging, and housing allocations should in fact be questioned. They are based on demographic studies which predict increasing numbers of small households. However, developers responding to the signals given by the housing market, continue to build unnecessarily large properties in locations where cars are essential for access to any facilities. In Surrey in 1986, for example, 36 per cent of new houses were detached properties, and although 74 per cent of households were only one or two person, only 54 per cent of the new properties were one- or two-bedroomed.

A revised Planning Policy Guidance Note on Housing was issued by the DoE in October 1989. It assumes that the housing shortage is due to land shortages, rather than this mismatch between real need and actual provision. In fact, more land is currently allocated in structure plans (on which planning permission has been or would be granted) than required by the DoE in every region. In England and Wales this land could provide for 23 per cent more dwellings than required by the DoE.

Both the Environment White Paper of September 1990

and the DoE's revised guidance on housing encourage local authorities to protect open spaces and gardens, but omit the necessary corollary, which is to insist on high density development of up to four or five storeys where development is permitted, to reduce the dependency of residents on cars. Much new development is at surburban population densities which are often inadequate to support a full range of local facilities such as shops, doctors' surgeries and pubs within walking distance. Such densities are also more resource intensive, requiring more construction materials and more infrastructure provision per person.

The issue of affordability is inadequately addressed. Provision for self-build housing has been limited and the levels of subsidy by the DoE for housing association schemes were cut to 75–80 per cent in 1989. This has made inner-city refurbishment (which requires around 85 per cent subsidy) uneconomical, even though such rehabilitation provides more appropriate housing at a lower environmental cost. The director of the National Federation of Housing Associations estimated that the proportion of housing association funds spent on refurbishment would fall from 50 per cent to 20 per cent as a result. Indeed, in Leicester, the number of rehabilitation schemes had fallen by 75 per cent between 1988/9 and 1989/90.

In rural areas there are other problems. In October 1989, the DoE's revised Planning Policy Guidance on the countryside and the rural economy proposed that land which would otherwise not be considered appropriate for development could be released for affordable housing. This is likely to include land of high nature conservation or landscape value such as at Wentnor in South Shropshire, where the proposed development lies in an Area of Outstanding Natural Beauty.

# Inner cities

Pressures in the city in some ways mirror those in the countryside. Short-term commercial interests often prevail over those of the environment – and of local people. Government strategy for inner city regeneration has often increased, not reduced, the problems.

The grandiose plan to build a barrage across Cardiff Bay to create a permanent lake, thereby 'improving' the environment for comprehensive office and residential re-development around the Bay, illustrates the effects of Government policy. The barrage would flood the entire Tiger Bay Site of Special Scientific Interest, the habitat of some 8,000 waders and waterfowl. Although initial plans to regenerate the Cardiff docklands had wide support, opposition has grown since the setting up in 1986 of the Cardiff Bay Development Corporation which is promoting the barrage scheme.

This Corporation was explicitly modelled on the London Docklands Development Corporation (LDDC), the best-known Urban Development Corporation (UDC), created in 1981 alongside the Mersey Development Corporation. More recently, despite criticism of the first two, nine further UDCs have been established. They have almost all been granted powers to operate in what the *Guardian* (March 30th 1990) called 'an unfettered developers' dream where the ordinary rules of planning are suspended' and where 'a market-led free-for-all was making fortunes for those quick to take a risk.'

What is at stake in Cardiff, and in many more city sites up and down the country, is not just the local environment but the Government's policies on inner city regeneration – policies subject to growing criticism. The Government's basic strategy has been to encourage private sector invest-ment in the inner city, through a mixture of public subsidy and relaxed planning rules. It believes this will lead to restoration of the built environment and the creation of local employment. The support provided has been focused on certain areas, notably the eleven Urban Development Areas (where the UDCs operate) and 57 inner city local authority areas where authorities receive funding under the Urban Programme.

# Urban regeneration policy

In 1988 the Prime Minister declared: 'The Government has a comprehensive approach to inner cities renewal, starting with site clearance and extending to help with improving sporting facilities and the cultural environment.' In fact her claim followed a period of effective disinvestment by government in the inner cities.

Between 1981 and 1988, a little over £2 billion of public money (at 1981 prices) was spent on urban regeneration, with just over a quarter going to the Urban Development Corporations. An optimistic estimate of the stimulated private sector investment is £9.25 billion. The figures look impressive. But they have to be set in the context of the Government's parallel *reduction* in rate support grant, a reduction which hit urban authorities particularly hard. The total cut in rate support grant (at 1981 prices) between 1979 and 1987 was £18 billion, and the 57 Urban Programme authorities alone lost £2 billion.

What did this mean on the ground? In Manchester, of a total of £148 million spent under the Urban Programme, the accumulated increases between 1981 and 1988 totalled just £10 million. If the Rate Support Grant had remained the same in real terms, the city would have received £278 million more than it actually did. Thus Manchester suffered an effective cut of £268 million. The threat of rate-capping meant that rates could not be increased to compensate and expenditure had to be cut (in real terms) across the range of local government services such as social services, transport and environmental health.

Moreover, the usefulness of the Urban Programme money for tackling inner city problems was reduced. Expenditure designed to increase private investment rose (from £178 million in 1979/80 to a projected 1988/9 figure of £475 million), while expenditure on social and community projects was cut (from £197 million to £118 million over the same period). Disadvantaged groups which have suffered from the enforced cuts in local services are certainly not being helped by this bias in favour of commercial interests. Even within the economic support goal of the Urban Programme, support for community business and cooperatives is still limited to £1,000 per company. Community businesses tend to pay more regard to environmental concerns than equivalent private companies. Indeed some operate directly to improve the environment, for example running home insulation programmes to conserve energy.

The value of the private sector money triggered by these subsidies must be questioned. Many investments have simply been attracted from other locations, bringing existing staff and purchasing networks with them. An official evaluation revealed deadweight (investment which would have occurred anyway) of around 30 per cent in the Urban Development Grant scheme. The quality and environmental impact of such new development is not effectively controlled (particularly in Urban Development Corporations). Above all, such investment by the private sector, although often generating physical development (new buildings), only has incidental benefits in tackling local deprivation, discrimination or environmental degradation. It is far less effective than expenditure aimed directly at these targets.

In 1988 the Government's Action for Cities initiative was

103

launched, repackaging the existing programmes on urban renewal with those on employment and training and revising grant regimes to create the City Grant system. This provided a series of business breakfasts around the country and just £100 million of new money.

# Urban Development Corporations and Housing Action Trusts

The Urban Development Corporations are at the heart of the Government's strategy for the inner city. Even in terms of their own objectives – 'to assemble land and cost-effectively trigger private sector investment in redevelopment of the built environment' – they have been unsuccessful. Only the London Docklands Development Corporation has attracted significant amounts of private investment, and even that has required high subsidies. A *Financial Times* report (April 19th 1990) on the London Docklands Development Corporation quoted developers as saying that it was in 'a parlous state'. Excessive bureaucracy and lack of clear aims were among the charges levelled at it and at the other UDCs.

The local government think tank, the Centre for Local Economic Strategies (CLES), published a report in March 1990 which gave an interim view of the UDCs' performance. CLES reported that there had been no systematic monitoring of the Corporations' success in creating local employment: the one exception to this rule, a LDDC assessment, came up with results described as 'not so far encouraging'. Most jobs 'created' were in fact transfers from one employer to another. Targetting of job creation is minimal: the LDDC does not even monitor the ethnic origin of its own employees.

In Leeds and other towns, as well as in London, small

and medium-sized firms have actually been compelled to close down under UDC land assembly and clearance schemes. Such schemes are seen as necessary because of the UDCs' emphasis on a large scale redevelopment, rather than small scale, locally based, refurbishment and re-development. The transfer of planning powers to the UDCs (in England) has led to approval for massive proposals, such as Canary Wharf, which are completely unrelated to existing and potential infrastructure.

The Docklands Consultative Committee, a local body supported by the local authorities of the Docklands area, recently published a highly critical eight-year review of the LDDC. 'Docklands', they conclude, 'is experiencing severe over-development, chronic congestion and a chaotic urban form precisely because a planned approach to its redevelopment has been ignored.' The lack of jobs created for the local unemployed is also stressed.

The LDDC has placed more emphasis on training and community concerns since 1988, and in 1989 announced a £51 million community spending programme. However, the DoE considers that it is not the function of the LDDC to fund social programmes. A leaked letter from a DoE civil servant states that 'it is important also to avoid the implication that LDDC has policies in fields such as health service provision.' The DoE is reported to have pressured the Corporation to reduce the social budget to £36 million in 1990/1 and to just £17 million in 1991/2.

The Centre for Local Economic Strategies also reported that many local authorities were uneasy about yielding their planning control to Government-appointed boards: 'Many local authorities told us they could do as well, and probably a lot better with their local experience, then the UDCs if they were given the resources of money and powers that UDCs were given. This is a crucial issue for local economic development.'

The major diversion of financial resources away from

locally-elected, publicly-accountable bodies towards centrally-imposed, undemocratic agencies such as the Urban Development Corporations is reflected in housing policy in the form of Housing Action Trusts (HATs). HATs were introduced by the Housing Act of 1988, and provide for 'problem' housing estates to be taken out of the control of the local authority, 'regenerated' by an independent board and then transferred to a private sector landlord or back to the council. Local resistance has so far defeated proposals for HATs in Sandwell, Leeds and Sunderland, while in Southwark, Lambeth and Waltham Forest decisions have yet to be made on whether to implement the proposals.

# Enterprise Zones

Meanwhile deliberate relaxations of planning regulations, intended to encourage private developers into particular areas, further weaken local authority powers. The 1980 Local Government Planning and Land Act introduced Enterprise Zones, which provided incentives for developers, including a rates 'holiday' and streamlined planning controls. Twenty-four such zones have been declared. Many of these are now dominated by low-rise retail and warehouse parks which compete with existing small business and local facilities. Simplified Planning Zones, introduced in the 1986 Housing and Planning Act, aim to further speed up the planning process where they are declared by local authorities. However, authorities have so far designated only a handful of such zones.

# Derelict land and contamination

Land in urban areas, particularly in central locations,

should be used efficiently to minimise the need for urban development on greenfield sites. However, in the UK there is over 40,000 hectares of derelict land, much of it in urban areas, and perhaps twice as much again of 'waste land' (not classified as derelict).

In 1987/8 only £81 million was spent on the derelict land programme, of which over £50 million was spent reclaiming 250 hectares for industrial and commercial use. The total area of derelict land was reduced only marginally between 1982 and 1988 and the area of derelict land in urban areas has if anything increased, with more 'general industrial' dereliction being generated than cleared.

The Government has focused attention on underused land in the public sector (local authorities and nationalised industries). Legislation was introduced in the 1980 Local Government, Planning and Land Act to create a public register of such land. Procedures introduced for enforcing sale of such land were streamlined by the Local Government Act of 1988.

No such pressure has been placed on land in private ownership, even though this constitutes over half of the derelict land in Britain. Legislation was passed in 1987 to open the Land Registry (which records the ownership of land on transfer) to public inspection. However, it has not yet been implemented and as it will not be retrospective, it will only permit inspection of data from transfers of ownership made after the Registry has been opened. Thus it will remain difficult to identify the owners of the vast majority of derelict sites.

The potential strategic value of many public sector sites has been ignored. Railheads will be vital when rail replaces road transport when the environmental costs of the latter become clearer. However, sites such as goods yards, sidings and embankments are being compulsorily sold and/or redeveloped. Moreover, 'derelict' land reclamation has destroyed sites of value for nature conservation. In

London, for example, of seven wasteland sites designated by the London Ecology Unit as of Metropolitan Importance for Nature Conservation, two were damaged and three destroyed between 1985 and 1988. The Unit recorded the loss of nine sites of conservation importance, and threats to 29 more, between 1984 and 1987, mainly due to the lack of protection provided for such sites by Government planning guidance.

The DoE derelict land policy review of 1989 responded to pressure from environmental groups and gave increased emphasis to the 'reclamation' of derelict land for open space or nature conservation use. However, ministerial approval for the policy changes has not yet been obtained, and the guidelines for derelict land grants have therefore yet to be revised accordingly.

Much urban wasteland may be contaminated with industrial pollution. Official figures, based on known previous uses, suggest around 65 per cent of such land in the UK as a whole, while one West Midlands study based on ground survey put the figure as high as 85 per cent. Restoring this land will not be cheap, whether for redevelopment or as an amenity for local people, plants and wildlife. But over the four-year period from 1987/8 to 1991/2, DoE spending on derelict land was scheduled to fall from fifteen per cent to ten per cent of the Urban Programme budget.

# Appropriate regeneration

The Government has promoted environmental improvement of inner cities, but only insofar as it makes the improved areas more attractive to commercial developers. The glossy 'Action for Cities' pamphlet said: 'A clean and well-maintained environment is vitally important to business confidence'. But local government and the voluntary sector have had to take most of the responsibility for carrying out even this environmental improvement work. Local government gets no additional resources to tackle many problems of environmental degradation. Some private sector development schemes have added to local problems, generating noise, disturbance and illegal tipping of waste, notably construction wastes.

In several cases, local people have tried to show the way forward in creating sensitive development, plans which would economically regenerate inner city areas while preserving and enhancing their environmental attractions. The Kirkstall Valley Campaign in Leeds is a well-known and persuasive case in point. The Valley was to have been obliterated by two superstores, 5,000 car parking spaces and a theme park. After months of effort and many public meetings, local residents produced their own alternative plan, which provided for new housing and industrial use (including a recycling and composting plant), but preserved the green spaces, allotments and wildlife of the Valley. The commercial development plan has been abandoned. But for every success or partial success there are innumerable local initiatives which get nowhere.

Government policy needs to support such local initiatives, rather than vesting power in unaccountable bodies and often giving priority to commercial considerations. Local involvement in planning must be supported by legislation requiring major developments to gain the involvement or approval of representative commmunity groups, or by financial support for the preparation of objections or alternative proposals.

# Planning permissions

In general, the Government has furthered the impression that the planning system is seen as little more than an encumbrance to the market. Development is seen as desirable in itself, and conservation is neglected. Increased weight is given to the 'presumption in favour of development'. Acceptable grounds for refusing planning applications have been ever more tightly defined, and in several recent cases developments running counter to adopted local and structure plans have been allowed on appeal when the developer has successfully argued that the plans are out of date.

Appeals by developers against the refusal of planning permission have become much more frequent, and have been upheld by the DoE in a growing number of cases. Between 1980 and 1987, the number of appeals made annually more than doubled, and the proportion of appeals upheld rose by nearly 20 per cent. An increasing number of appeals were successful even in specially protected areas: in 1988/9, no less than 104 appeals (33 per cent of the total, as against 25 per cent in similar cases in 1980/1) were upheld in designated National Parks.

A significant number of local authorities have been losing claims made against them by developers for the award of costs. Many councillors are concerned that, following the guidance given in a 1987 DoE circular, they may even find themselves personally liable to surcharges if they take decisions counter to Government policy.

These trends have undermined the notion of 'positive planning' - planning which promotes the meeting of local and wider needs, rather than planning which merely restrains commercial demands in the extreme cases. This is especially unfortunate at a time when there has been an accelerating trend of land-use change. After a sharp decline during the 1970s, the spread of urban areas stabilised during the early 1980s, and it is now speeding up again. Between 1985 and 1989, the rate of urban sprawl increased by 21 per cent to cover around 6,500 hectares per year.

The Government's hostility towards the positive planning principle was clearly expressed in the significantly entitled *Lifting the Burden* White Paper of 1986, which argued that the planning system 'imposes costs on the economy and constraints on enterprise that are not always justified by any real public benefit in the individual case.'

The environmental costs imposed on society by development have not been recognised, nor have proposals for changes to the development control procedure to take account of them been implemented by the Government. Local authorities have been urged instead to speed up their decisions and to minimise conditions attached to planning permissions. The DoE's Efficient Planning document of July 1989 proposed that local authorities might extend locally the range of developments permitted under the general development order, which defines developments permitted without any application for permission. However, the document made some other more positive proposals, such as putting forward the idea that repetitive applications might be turned away. These proposals have not as yet been converted into legislation or guidance.

# Environmental Impact Assessment

Concern about the environmental impact of major developments in many parts of Europe led to European Commission proposals for statutory Environmental Impact Assessment. These were long resisted by the UK, but in 1985 a Directive was finally agreed.

When Britain implemented the Directive in July 1988, it tried to limit its application to major industrial developments. This was in line with a DoE working party report of 1985, which had stated that the Government would aim at 'minimising. . . additional burdens. . . on developers'.

Pressure from the Commission forced a change of policy, but the relevant regulations still only meet the absolute minimum required by the Directive.

Nonetheless, more environmental assessments have been carried out than the DoE had expected. In the eighteen months to December 1989, 143 Environmental Statements were submitted. However, where developers have disputed requests for Environmental Statements made by the planning authority, the DoE has held to its policy of minimising burdens: in only 39 per cent of these cases were directions made requiring a Statement to be submitted.

Some of the Statements prepared have been of limited value. When a sample of such Statements was analysed by the Environmental Impact Assessment centre at the University of Manchester, only 25 per cent were found to be adequate according to a strict interpretation of the Directive. But the DoE has yet to state categorically that an inadequate Statement is grounds for the refusal of planning permission. The Environment White Paper failed even to recognise these problems, and simply proposed further evaluation of the process.

# Permitted use rights in the countryside

Farmers and land owners have 'permitted use rights' (rights to develop without going through the normal planning procedures) on agricultural land. In many cases such development should not in fact be permitted on environmental grounds. It also tends to be of lower quality just because planning permission does not have to be sought in the normal way.

However, proposals have actually been made to extend

the exceptions enjoyed by agricultural development. The 1989 DoE consultation paper *Permitted Use Rights in the Countryside* suggested that planning and land-use restrictions should be lifted for a range of additional activities. Existing agricultural buildings, exempt from controls, could have been converted or replaced. Such developments as caravan sites and theme parks could have gone ahead without any need for planning permission.

Fortunately, unanimous opposition from conservation and other groups forced the withdrawal of these proposals. However the subsequent revision of the DoE's Countryside and Rural Economy Planning Policy Guidance Note (December 1989) still apparently enshrined the view that the planning system acts as an undesirable constraint on economic development, and in particular on farm diversification. It was suggested that the redundancy criterion (preventing conversion of farm buildings to other uses so long as they were still required for agriculture) should be removed, allowing the use of the buildings to be changed. An additional new building for the agricultural use could then be constructed under permitted development rights. Although control over siting, design and external appearance of new agricultural buildings was proposed in the Environment White Paper, the root problems of permitted development were not addressed.

The Government has also weakened the protection fórmerly given to agricultural land for the sake of food production. In 1987, the right of the Ministry of Agriculture, Fisheries and Food to be consulted on development proposals was curtailed. The MAFF is now only asked to comment on proposals that involve more than twenty hectares of high-grade farm land.

# Demolition

Demolition of buildings generally does not constitute

development. Therefore it does not require planning permission, except in the case of listed buildings or buildings in conservation areas. This often leads to the wasteful loss of still-useful buildings, as well as adversely affecting activities which do not yield high rents even though they may be of value to the local community.

Speculative demolition has occurred where permission for redevelopment might well not otherwise have been granted.

Following the rejection of three Private Members' Bills on this topic, the DoE finally produced a consultation document in 1990. However, this only covered dwelling-houses. Nor did the DoE announce any definite intention to produce guidance or regulation on the matter.

Demolition and redevelopment are further encouraged at the expense of rehabilitation because VAT is charged on refurbishment, but not on new construction.

# Special Development Orders and Planning Agreements

The Secretary of State for the Environment can make use of Special Development Orders to grant general permission for a particular type of development. The present Government has at times made use of them to avoid public debate. In 1986, for example, a Special Development Order was used to force through proposals for exploratory investigations of possible sites for low-level radioactive waste dumping.

Section 52 Planning Agreements are another administrative device whose use has worried environmental campaigners. Under the Town and Country Planning Acts, local authorities may employ them in negotiating with developers, in order to obtain a gain which will ameliorate the effect of a development but which cannot reasonably be imposed by a planning condition. The problem is that such agreements have been abused to gain permissions which should never have been granted.

Many people, including MPs, also feel that local authorities have been unduly reluctant to make use of them to insist on benefits: for instance Robin Squire MP, a member of the House of Commons Environment Committee, recently called on planning authorities to use agreements to get retailers to install recycling deposit facilities.

The Government produced a consultation paper on Planning Agreements in July 1989. It addressed neither of these concerns, proposing instead that developers should be allowed to offer planning gains unilaterally, rather than negotiating them with local authorities. The DoE Inspector at an appeal would then decide whether the offer was appropriate. The implicit danger is that such unilateral offers will be made in order to propose inducements unrelated to the actual development plan, again raising the fear that entirely unsuitable schemes may be approved in consequence.

Revised guidance was again promised in the Environment White Paper, but only to clarify that agreements *may* include provisions to compensate for the loss of *existing* resources or amenities *on* the development site (our emphasis) – an extremely limited interpretation.

# Metropolitan and regional strategic planning

The county structure plan system, which has evolved over time, has always embodied a major element of positive planning, guiding development to where it is needed.

The development planning system in metropolitan areas

had to be revised on the abolition of the Metropolitan County Councils and the GLC in 1985. A new system of Unitary Development Plans (UDPs), drawn up by the district authorities in line with guidance issued by the Secretary of State for the Environment, has now been introduced.

The guidance document issued has been widely criticised. In the case of London, the carefully-prepared advice of the all-party London Planning Advisory Committee was ignored. Drawn up while Nicholas Ridley was Secretary of State, the guidance document was issued by his successor Chris Patten on the last day of the Parliamentary session. It fails to integrate land-use planning with transport, neglects environmental problems, and requires the boroughs to cater to market-generated development proposals. In particular, it rejects the Advisory Committee's recommendation that new commercial development should be concentrated at sites spread across London (within existing limits of the built-up area) and accessible by public transport, rather than in the centre or on the fringes where it will lead to traffic congestion.

The guidance document was described by the President of the Royal Town Planning Institute as 'at best complacent and at the worst a dereliction of the Government's responsibility for the strategic planning of our capital city.'

The Unitary Development Plan experience is not a hopeful precedent for those concerned about the likely impact of Government proposals (contained in the DoE's 1989 White Paper on the *Future of Development Plans*) to abolish county structure plans. It is suggested that strategic guidance should henceforth be issued by the DoE. This is likely to be a retrograde step, since, on the whole, county structure plans show more concern for the environment than do either the DoE's strategic guidance document or district council Local Plans.

Other undesirable effects of the proposed change include

the much greater task that will face voluntary organisations and statutory bodies such as the Nature Conservancy Council, who will be expected to comment on a much greater number of Plans without being given more resources to do so. Moreover, developers can usually bring pressure to bear more effectively on District than on County Councils.

Guidance has already been issued to begin the process by which county structure plans will be slimmed down into statements of county planning policy. A narrower range of topics will be covered and developers will be subject to less direct influence from the revised plans. In the DoE's White Paper of November 1989, environmental topics falling within the scope of the revised plans were limited to 'Green Belts and conservation in town and country'. The integration of environmental concerns with other policy areas was not suggested.

The Government's intention to introduce statutory district plans was reiterated in the Environment White Paper of 1990, which also contained outlines for streamlining procedures for the adoption of plans. This will almost inevitably reduce the ability of the public to influence the content of development plans.

# Private and Hybrid Bills

Notoriously, there was no Public Inquiry into the Channel Tunnel – one of the most massive civil engineering projects in history, which will immediately affect hundreds of thousands of people. Instead, local objectors were invited to voice their views at a series of public Parliamentary sessions.

Unfortunately, this was just one striking example of a worrying new trend. Under the present Government, Private (and Hybrid) Bills have been used repeatedly to promote developments and avoid challenge by the normal planning process. In 1988/9 twice as many Private Bills came before Parliament as in 1987/8. Most of these related to transport infrastructure. Private Bills have been used to approve extensions of Felixstowe port, developments which have severely damaged an estuary Site of Special Scientific Interest. British Rail has sought to use a Private Bill to override control procedures for listed buildings at the King's Cross development site. The procedure has been subject to widespread criticism: John Wakeham MP described it as 'apparently arcane and complex'. In 1987, a Joint Committee was appointed to examine the procedure. In 1988, this recommended that public local inquiries should replace Private Bills for development proposals. The Government's immediate response was negative, retaining the basis of the Private Bill procedure, but attempting to speed it up. But in June 1990, a DoE consultation document was issued proposing the use of an Order procedure which would in most cases allow the public to be heard and their views considered at a local public inquiry. However, the Hybrid Bill procedure is not to be reformed, and could still be used to bypass the planning procedure.

*Friends of the Earth Policy Recommendations*
# ⸻ Planning and Inner Cities ⸻

1.   Financial support for inner city regeneration should be targeted on locally based economic development. Opportunities must be provided for increased community involvement.

2.   Environmental conditions must be imposed

(relating to building materials, energy standards and the like) where subsidies or loans are being provided (for instance through the City Grant or Urban Programme, or via Urban Development Corporations).

**3.** Incentives for re-use of land and rehabilitation of buildings should be improved. Specific measures should include increased support for the derelict land programme and for housing association rehabilitation; and the charging of VAT on materials for new buildings as well as on materials for refurbishment.

**4.** The accountability of Urban Development Corporations must be increased. Their programmes must be made subject to comprehensive environmental and social assessment.

**5.** The presumption against development in green belts should be extended to all greenfield sites.

**6.** The issues that can be considered in development control ('material considerations') should be extended to include issues such as energy demand and traffic generation so that sustainable development can be promoted.

**7.** Strategic and regional guidance and planning policy guidance should be revised to require positive promotion of sustainable development. In particular, guidance should stress the need for appropriate, high densities, rather than suburban densities, in town centres, and the need to keep central functions in the centre.

**8.** All demolition should be brought within the definition of development. The scope of use classes should also be reduced, particularly to prevent uncontrolled conversion from light industrial to office use, but also to assist in the retention of local facilities.

**9.** Agricultural, forestry and water company operations and developments should be included in the system of planning controls.

**10.** Valuable open land in urban areas should be protected by the creation of planning designations (with statutory weight) as 'open land' or 'conservation sites'.

**11.** Environmental Impact Assessments should be improved and extended to cover all currently discretionary projects, to require coverage of alternative ways of meeting need, and to require post-development study comparing effects with predicted impacts. The standard of environmental statements should be improved by encouraging planning authorities to reject applications automatically if the environmental statement is inadequate.

**12.** Procedures for consideration of major projects should be reformed. Private Bills should be replaced with public inquiries; third-party appeal against development control decisions should be allowed; funding for objectors at inquiries should be provided; the scope for public meetings should be widened; and less adversarial practices within inquiries should be promoted.

## Chapter 6

# ROADS TO NOWHERE: OUR TRANSPORT POLICY

During 1989, the number of vehicles on Britain's roads increased by 4 per cent to a record total of 24.2 million. The great majority (19 million) were cars, up by over 800,000 on the previous year.

It is against the background of figures such as these – from the annual Department of Transport census – that we must assess the recent Government announcement that spending on roads and motorways is to be doubled. Private cars and lorries are to be favoured. One more attempt is to be made, despite the long record of failure, to ease traffic congestion by road construction. Transport Secretary Nicholas Ridley described himself as unashamedly pro-motorist in 1984, and one of his most recent successors, Paul Channon, showed that he held identical views when in 1989 he launched a ten-year, £12 billion roads programme.

Meanwhile, British Rail has been subject to ever tighter financial constraints. Deregulation of buses has led to declining passenger numbers. Local councils have been forbidden to use central government grants to subsidise public transport.

121

In a word, Britain does not have a transport policy. It has a roads policy, a cars and lorries policy.

We know the social and environmental consequences. Landscapes and habitats are lost under concrete and tarmac. Vehicle exhausts spew out more and more greenhouse gases. Those who cannot afford, or do not want, their own cars find it harder and harder to move about. Pedestrians, cyclists and people living near busy roads face rising levels of noise, vibration and pollution, as well as increased risk of traffic accidents.

The environmental impact of transport was much discussed in the White Paper, *This Common Inheritance*. Despite the recognition of problems and possible solutions, such as light-rail systems, improved public transport, fuel taxation and increased fuel efficiency, the Government steadfastly avoided any firm commitments to regulation or increased investment.

# Roads, cars, lorries

Growing traffic congestion – most notoriously on the M25, that textbook case of how building big new roads can actually *cause* snarl-ups; growing public resistance to urban traffic and to the bulldozing of highways across the countryside; a growing scientific consensus on the imminent danger of the greenhouse effect . . . The circumstances are right for a shift in policy away from motor vehicle transport.

However, the 1990 Budget showed little sign of such a shift. Nigel Lawson, then Chancellor of the Exchequer, had halved subsidy on company cars in 1988–89, and reduced it by another 30 per cent the following year. This subsidy is a perk to employees from their employers which is funded by the tax-payer to the tune of over £2 billion a year. The further cut announced by Mr Lawson's successor, John Major, was of just 20 per cent. This was equivalent to a tax increase 'way ahead of inflation', commented an article in the *Independent* (March 21st 1990), 'but considerably less than the doubling of the charge that had been widely expected . . . Those who enjoy the benefits of having a company car must be happy to have escaped so lightly.' The cash value of company cars remains exempt from National Insurance levies on either employer or employee – a subsidy worth around 10 per cent of the car's cost to the firm providing it. Supposedly, the Government is committed to discouraging company car use, but little resolve to do so was shown on this occasion.

One welcome step taken in 1990 was the abandonment of the proposed £2 billion London road upgrading scheme. This was replaced by a much more modest £250 million programme. A tunnel from Chiswick to Wandsworth, large projects on the South Circular Road and A23 improvements were all dropped in the face of sustained protests by pressure groups and local residents. Encouragingly, the new Environment Secretary Chris Patten was reported to have opposed the original plans. It was also encouraging that further studies were announced into rail and underground projects, including an extension of the London underground Northern Line.

In May 1990, Transport Secretary Cecil Parkinson revealed a programme to cut the toll of road injuries to children, which have recently been running at 6,900 fatalities and serious injuries per year. Speed limits of 20 mph are likely to be applied by local authorities as a result of a Department of Transport move to cut the number of such accidents on the road. The use of road humps and chicanes (which reduce straight line travel and so speed) and the widening of footpaths were among measures which local authorities were urged to adopt to reduce vehicle speeds.

Many towns and cities on the continent, especially in the Netherlands and West Germany, are implementing much more comprehensive 'traffic calming' schemes to make roads safe for residents and pedestrians and discourage car use in urban areas.

There is little sign that the Department of Transport is ready to rethink its underlying commitment to road traffic. The doubling of expenditure on roads announced in the summer of 1989 was part of a long-term trend. Whereas Kenneth Clarke, then Junior Transport Minister, announced in 1981 that the motorway programme was coming to an end, his successors have made a virtue of their zeal for road building. In 1985, Nicholas Ridley boasted that Government spending on national roads had risen by 30 per cent in real terms since 1979. Then in 1989 Paul Channon, in his last ministerial post as Transport Secretary, published the White Paper *Roads to Prosperity* with its proposal to double spending – a strategy enthusiastically adopted by Cecil Parkinson, his successor.

The more recent White Paper, *This Common Inheritance*, did virtually nothing to control the increasing growth in traffic and consequent congestion. Most notably, the Government still sees road building as a solution, flying in the face of any attempts to control the growing contribution to greenhouse gases and destruction of the environment. The Government set no targets to control traffic growth, and in fact welcomed 'continuing widening of car ownership'. By contrast, Holland's Government has set a maximum target of a 35 per cent increase in traffic by 2010, half that expected without action.

# Rural environmental costs

As we have seen in the section on the countryside, rural environments have been and are being seriously threatened by the 'roads at any price' line of the Department of Transport.

The White Cliffs of Dover, the Peak District National Park, Oxleas Wood in south London (a large area of ancient woodland due to be hacked down for the sake of the East London River Crossing), the South Downs outside Brighton, Twyford Down in Hampshire – these are just a few of the better-known examples. The occasional reprieve, such as the decision to spare butterfly-rich Bernwood Forest, which lay in the path of the proposed M40 extension, is rightly a cause for rejoicing, but still leaves a dismal picture.

In 1985, a Friends of the Earth report showed that no less than 110 Sites of Special Scientific Interest risked partial –and in some cases, total – destruction by actual and projected road building during the 1980s and 1990s. The Council for the Protection of Rural England (CPRE) recently stated that Government policy meant 'increasing traffic, faster speeds and more heavy lorries' in the countryside. Commenting on the White Cliffs road scheme, a CPRE representative told the *Times* (April 16th 1990): 'If the Government regards the need for a new road as absolute, and such environmental treasures as expendable, its credibility as the steward of our inheritance will be ruined along with the White Cliffs.'

# Heavy lorries

Heavy lorries are a major cause of damage to roads. According to a National Audit Office report on heavy lorries, published in 1987, heavy lorries are responsible for between 72 per cent and 98 per cent of the structural damage to the roads. They also cause great stress and annoyance to those living near the roads they use. The Government's own Assessment Studies, carried out between 1985 and 1989, have indicated their unpopularity with Londoners. However, there is no sign of any strategy either to keep lorries away from residential areas or to keep their size within reasonable limits.

Indeed, permitted lorry weights (including cargoes) were increased from 32.5 to 38 tonnes after the 1983 general election. After 1999, they will rise again, to 40 tonnes, though this is due to a European initiative.

The Government has been notably lax in maintaining, monitoring and enforcing controls on lorry operators. A confidential Freight Transport Association report, leaked to Friends of the Earth in February 1989, indicated that existing environmental standards were likely to be loosened in the regulations controlling operation and use of heavy vehicles.

Enforcement measures to compel compliance with weight limits are years behind schedule, although the technology exists. For example, road sensors placed in the bed of the road can detect over-laden vehicles. Much stricter controls need to be mounted at ports. However, the Department of Transport has issued instructions that overloads of up to 10 per cent should not lead to prosecution. Checks on heavy lorries for speeding and overloading have declined. Foreign operators who break British law are not taken to court. Domestic operators now face on-the-spot fines of just £12: the previous average fine was £129. This is a direct result of Government policy.

# Urban public transport and bus deregulation

Enormous sums can be found for road building, but public transport in Britain is starved of resources. This affects both British Rail, whose case we discuss below, and other public transport bodies. The Transport Support Grant, the main method of distributing central government assistance

126

for local authority transport spending, explicitly prohibits local councils from using the money to support public transport.

London illustrates the results of this short-sighted attitude. The city's transport problems worsen from month to month. Yet since the Government took over responsibility for subsidising London Regional Transport, funding has halved to £48 million. It was set to fall further, until the King's Cross fire, which killed 31 people, and subsequent Inquiry revealed that standards of safety and maintenance were already dangerously inadequate.

The Confederation of British Industry has given examples of six companies which estimate joint losses of about £30 million a year in London alone due to road congestion. Royal Mail Letters estimated costs of £10.4 million due to traffic congestion, and British Telecom reckoned on an extra £7.25 million. The Confederation called for a Minister for Transport for London and the designation of the capital as a transport priority zone.

London's public transport network is clearly under-subsidised in world terms. In 1985, the subsidy stood at 30 per cent of costs. Almost every other western metropolis scored higher. Some figures for comparison: Paris 54 per cent, Los Angeles 69 per cent, Amsterdam 80 per cent, Rome 81 per cent.

Outside London, in both urban and rural areas, the deregulation of bus services has been the Government's major transport initiative. This was always a risky venture, owing as much to free market ideology as to an assessment of needs and priorities. Would operators compete for rush-hour times and densely populated routes, leaving empty spaces on the map and in timetables? Would they cut costs by buying older, cheaper vehicles – which would also be dirtier and less safe? Would they run all the registered services they had undertaken to provide? Nicholas Ridley was sanguine. 'Who needs evidence,' he asked, 'when you are blazing a trail?'

The trail has been blazed. The evidence is coming in, much of it gathered by the government-run Transport and Road Research Laboratory. And the indications are that deregulation has largely been a failure.

Increased minibus use, sometimes cited as one benefit of the change, was in fact already evident before deregulation. Bus mileage has increased, but passenger numbers have fallen. In the metropolitan areas outside London patronage has fallen by 15.2 per cent. Subsidy levels have also declined. There have been some hefty fare increases: 100 per cent on Merseyside, 238 per cent in South Yorkshire. Staff have faced wage cuts.

It is significant that deregulation has not yet been introduced in London. The Department of Transport would seem to be aware of the potential problems if minibuses proliferated and coherent centralised strategic planning gave way to a market scramble. The date on which London is to receive the blessings of deregulation seems to be continually deferred, but the plans have not been totally shelved. The Government now say that deregulation will be introduced in London after the next election.

# British Rail

Nationally, the Department of Transport employs some 10,000 people licensing, testing and taxing motor vehicles (though it still manages to lose more than £100 million a year in unpaid license duty, refusing to switch to the simpler and environmentally preferable option of increasing fuel tax and scrapping excise duty). A further 2,500 or so work in the road transport sphere. How many Department of Transport staff have jobs connected with the railways? Just 72.

Britain has consistently underfunded its rail network, and the present Government has made things worse by

128

placing British Rail under extremely tight financial constraints, setting it the toughest targets found in any industralised country.

Comparison with other European systems highlights BR's underfunding. Levels of subsidy are three times as high in France and six times as high in West Germany. In the summer of 1987, extra central government cash helped Swiss Railways boost passenger services by 12 per cent and offer new half-price reductions 24 hours a day to railcard holders. At this same time, BR (along with London Regional Transport) was announcing fare increases – to *discourage* rail travel!

Lack of subsidy and lack of investment mean that the service is ill-equipped for expansion. In Britain, we 'invest in' roads, but we 'subsidise' railways – according to the Government, who of course dislike subsidy. Rail has to provide an 'economic return' after covering the costs not only of staff and rolling stock, but also of track maintenance and replacement. Roads suffer from no comparable restraint. Even to invest sizeable sums of its own money, BR must await government approval. Long delays in much-needed programmes result.

Only in February 1989 did the long-planned King's Lynn electrification get the go-ahead, which will bring faster services and reduce noise and air pollution from locomotives. Yet with only 29 per cent of its track electrified, BR is once again bottom of the western European league.

BR is being lined up for privatisation. Detailed proposals, when they are published, must be carefully scrutinised for their likely environmental impact. One worry is that a privatised railway would concentrate on profitable business lines. On less profitable routes, rising fares and falling standards might force people off the railway and back into their cars.

# Planning

Two questions, in particular, need asking about the transport planning process. In the first place, are the right questions asked and the right criteria employed? And secondly, is the system open and democratic?

At present, the answer to both questions is a resounding 'No'.

The form of cost/benefit analysis used to decide on the viability of roads estimates how many people would use the road, what savings in travelling time would be achieved, and what economic benefit should be assigned. The Government's own studies, prepared by the Standing Advisory Committee on Trunk Road Assessment, show that if such cost/benefit analysis is applied to railways, they show far more benefit than almost all roads. Yet the Government takes the line that such analysis is not appropriate for railways because they earn revenue from their passengers.

This is an important and unwarrantable source of bias. The logic of the Pearce Report's proposals for a Green Tax implies that the same yardstick should be used whether road or rail is under consideration.

Where the economic case is weak despite this built-in bias, the Department of Transport has been known simply to recalculate the figures. This happened in the Inquiry into the East London River Crossing. When proceedings had been going on for 134 days, the initial sums were revised, and £14.5 million in new benefits was suddenly found. At the click of a calculator, a loss-making project became profitable. The Department of Transport made such adjustments no less than three times during the Inquiry.

Transport planners have actually been banned from using a computer model specially designed to analyse London's transport problems. The 'London Area Model' was withdrawn by the Department of Transport in May 1988 and the London Planning Advisory Committee told to stop using it. Assessing four alternative strategies, the model chose to charge motorists for road use and channel the revenue back into public transport. Not only did this emerge as the most effective solution, it was also the only alternative to show a profit. The model also indicated that the Government's preferred strategy – eliminating rail subsidy, halving subsidy to bus passengers, and investing in substantial new road building – was the worst option of all.

Planning procedures are undemocratic, as well as flawed. Public inquiries into road schemes cannot hear objections bearing on the need for new roads, they can only debate their routing. The Department, in time-honoured White-hall fashion, is both judge and jury: it organises the proceedings, and decides their outcome. Government forecasts are treated as policy and cannot be challenged, even though they often rest on dubious assumptions about economic growth and contentious notions of what would be a desirable outcome.

Particular anger was aroused when Nicholas Ridley, as Transport Secretary, ignored constitutional convention and overrode an all-party Parliamentary Committee to force the Okehampton Bypass through Dartmoor National Park, defying in the process both local opinion and stated policy on National Parks. He was able to ignore these viewpoints because none were legally binding, although such overwhelming hostility to a scheme might normally be expected to influence the Minister responsible.

Further violations and infringements of democracy are discussed in the section on the countryside. The use of Private Bills has been a particularly worrying development. Most notoriously of all, the Channel Tunnel and its associated high speed rail link went ahead without any public inquiry, even though this constitutes the largest civil engineering project in British history.

*Friends of the Earth Policy Recommendations*

# Transport

1.   The public inquiry system for new roads should be drastically reformed. For every new scheme, there should be a thorough traffic appraisal and economic evaluation, and a full assessment of environmental and social impacts.

2.   Public transport (including light rail, bus and rail services) should be assessed on equal terms with road building schemes.

3.   The tax subsidy for company cars should be abolished at the next budget. (*Reiterated as 'Air Pollution' Policy Recommendation #4, 'Global Warming' Policy Recommendation #5*]

4.   Vehicle Excise Duty should be scrapped and incorporated into petrol tax. [*Reiterated as 'Global Warming' Policy Recommendation #7*]

5.   Lower speed limits should be introduced in urban areas. Local authorities should be financially assisted by the Government to enable the introduction of traffic calming measures to promote road safety and environmental improvements in street design.

6.   There should be no cuts in the British Rail network.

7.   Regulations and taxation policy should be used to improve freight transport efficiency and road-pricing should be introduced for heavy lorries. The latter could be in the form of a charge for heavy vehicles entering sensitive areas such as town centres, using detectors in the carriageway. The Government should take effective measures to shift freight from road to rail.

**8.** Public transport systems should be adequately funded in order to encourage their widest possible use, giving the public a real choice in how to get from A to B.

**9.** The expanded £12 billion (1989 prices) national road building programme should be scrapped.

# Chapter 7

# POLLUTION CONTROL

Much of this book is concerned with pollution control. We discuss the problems arising in various enviromental fields, the measures necessary to meet those problems, and the adequacy (or inadequacy) of government action hitherto.

It is worth looking specifically at the wider legislative and institutional framework for pollution control. The Government has introduced some significant changes, many of them useful, at least in principle. However, much remains to be done. The current framework is still too fragmented to coordinate the unified strategic response which the task demands.

Important recent developments have included the laying of the foundation for 'Integrated Pollution Control' in the Environmental Protection Act. Given the fact that as recently as November 1988, Nicholas Ridley was telling viewers of the BBC TV programme *Panorama* that no parliamentary time could be guaranteed for pollution control legislation, the mere fact of legislation indicates a welcome shift of Government thinking.

## Her Majesty's Inspectorate of Pollution

In August 1986, the Department of the Environment

announced the establishment of a unified pollution inspectorate for England and Wales: Her Majesty's Inspectorate of Pollution (HMIP). This was a belated move, first recommended by the Royal Commission on Environmental Pollution (RCEP) some eleven years previously.

In 1976, the RCEP had suggested that the new body be an expansion of the existing Alkali Inspectorate (later to become the Industrial Air Pollution Inspectorate), and that it should operate within the Department of the Environment, rather than within the Health and Safety Executive, as the Alkali Inspectorate did. The RCEP clearly saw a need for an approach to pollution control which would embrace industrial processes and the disposal of waste to air, land and water. The control of discharges to different media by separate bodies had led to a blinkered outlook. For instance, the Industrial Air Pollution Inspectorate had no duty to consider further the consequences of reduction of air emissions, even though removal of an air pollution problem could merely lead to a pollution in water or on land. The Commission had received evidence on the removal of fluoride from a waste gas stream. The fluoride was filtered from the gas with a wet filter. The liquid from the filter was subsequently discharged to a sewer and sewage treatment works. Sewage sludge from the treatment plant was spread on land, where grazing cattle became ill from consuming too much fluoride.

By unifying the regulators, the Commission envisaged that disposal by 'best practicable means' would become disposal by 'best practicable environmental option'. The Government initially rejected the RCEP'S view in its response – which came six years later.

Eventually, however, Her Majesty's Inspectorate of Pollution (HMIP) was established, in April 1987, by bringing together the inspectorates for air, water and radiochemicals.

The early history of HMIP has been beset with staffing

problems. When it was established with a complement of 214 posts, there were 66 vacancies. A year later, there were still 32 vacancies.

The root cause is lack of money. Sufficient staff with the necessary expertise and industrial experience could simply not be recruited for the salaries offered. After two years, the Department of the Environment recognised this, and announced salary increases in the range of 16 to 28 per cent. A recruitment drive was launched at the end of 1989 for new pollution inspectors. In January 1990, David Trippier, Minister of State for the Environment, revealed in answer to a Parliamentary question that 41 out of 240 posts were still vacant. But in May 1990, Chris Patten acknowledged that 44 positions (out of 250) remained vacant. In the meantime, morale and staff numbers have been severely damaged at HMIP. Four leading officials have resigned. One of them had called for the number of waste inspectors to be doubled.

Under the Environmental Protection Act, HMIP is to implement Integrated Pollution Control, which was originally scheduled to begin to take effect in January 1991.

# Integrated Pollution Control

In July 1988, a Department of the Environment consultation paper was issued on Integrated Pollution Control (IPC), proposing that technology-based controls be applied to waste streams from scheduled industrial sites. It was envisaged that major air polluters, dischargers of 'Red List' substances to water (see the chapter on Water Pollution), and producers of 'large amounts of special wastes' would be included. The controls, at an estimated 5,000 sites, will cover processes such as those at cement works, the pesticide and pharmaceutical industries, chemical fertiliser factories, chemical incinerators, iron and steel works, and fuel-burning power plants.

About 500 sites will come under the jurisdiction of HMIP when dischargers of any of the 23 Red List substances are included. The Red List includes the weedkillers atrazine and simazine and the timber preservatives pentachlorophenol and tributyl tin oxide. Chemicals on the List are those which have been judged to pose the greatest threat to the aquatic environment because of their toxicity, tendency to concentrate in food chains, and resistance to breaking down in the environment into less toxic compounds.

Atmospheric emissions from the scheduled sites are currently regulated by HMIP, but under the old system. Industrialists have to operate in accordance with 'best practicable means', with notes from HMIP as guidance. Standards set in the notes for the maximum quantities of pollutants to be emitted are not legally binding, but can be used by HMIP as a yard-stick for judging the operation of the plant. For example, sulphur dioxide emissions from power stations will be controlled by the use of flue gas desulphurisation equipment which should enable the stations to comply with the emission standards in the relevant guidance note.

Critics of the system have been concerned that the guidance notes were written in consultation with industry. The Department of the Environment has promised that consultation with the public will be a feature of the new guidance notes for Integrated Pollution Control. These new notes will identify standards for emissions according to the 'best available techniques not entailing excessive cost' (known as 'batneec').

Operators of prescribed processes, such as those listed above, will have to apply for authorisation permits for discharges from new or altered works. For older works, IPC will be brought in on a phased basis. This may allow some works to continue operating under the older system for a considerable time before being made subject to all the requirements of the IPC scheme.

The implementation of batneec standards does not necessarily mean *minimisation* of emissions, in the sense of reducing them to the minimum possible. The Department of the Environment has made it quite clear that financial considerations will still feature in IPC. The phrase 'not entailing excessive costs' may cause many arguments, pitting environmental protection against industrial profits. However, statements from the Department have indicated that HMIP and industry will have to consider the use of all 'available' technology, not necessarily that in general use or just that which is available in the UK.

It remains to be seen how effective the new IPC regime will be in actually reducing harmful or potentially harmful emissions. The IPC guidance notes issued to industry will only become available as HMIP produces them. Encouragingly, a time-table for implementation has been proposed. It has already been revised once to give both HMIP, which still faces a huge task with its small workforce, and industry longer to prepare. Initial implementation of IPC for new processes and large combustion plants has been delayed by three months, and incorporation of older existing works and processes into the system will begin fifteen months later than originally anticipated. HMIP will still have to continue current duties such as site visits, but will also need to vet applications and issue authorisation for the scheduled processes, while identifying the standards appropriate for 'best available techniques not entailing excessive cost'.

Local authorities will become responsible for air emissions from less complex industrial processes or those with relatively minor outputs of waste gases, including such operations as scrap metal recovery, crematoria, vehicle paint spraying, particle board manufacture and clinical waste incineration. The lists and threshold figures for deciding whether a process is authorised by HMIP have not been finalised yet, but it has been estimated that about 25,000 processes will be controlled eventually by local authorities, principally district councils.

Local authorities may well lack both resources and expertise. According to an ENDS (Environmental Data Services) Report, Government estimates of total costs to be incurred by local authorities have been disputed. The figure of £0.5 million may well underestimate a more significant financial burden to local authorities. If they are to find resources to do the job, local authorities must be allowed to charge realistic fees to the companies they are monitoring.

Another important feature of IPC and the Environmental Protection Act will be the establishment of public registers. This will allow public scrutiny of applications for and monitoring and enforcement of any prescribed processes, and so increase accountability. Registers of monitoring data for effluent discharges to rivers, groundwater and coastal waters have been available since August 1985, and the increased accessibility of information about air pollution, discharges of Red List substances to sewers, and other prescribed processes is welcome.

Much of the detail of IPC implementation will emerge only as future Regulations are issued by the Government. Acts in themselves do not necessarily mean great change. A minister may be granted powers by a law, but it can then be a matter for policy whether those powers are actually used. For instance, the Control of Pollution Act 1974 enabled the establishment of public registers detailing water quality (excluding drinking water quality), but the relevant sections were not brought into force until 1984. The registers themselves were not set up until August 1985.

# Fragmentation and other problems

Even after these overdue reforms, Britain lacks the unified, powerful pollution control agency we need. HMIP might eventually become such an agency, not unlike the US Environmental Protection Agency, with wide scope and correspondingly wide powers. HMIP, however, will have to integrate its own four divisions before it can properly implement and expand the concept of integrated pollution control.

Structural problems still persist – foremost among them the problem of fragmented responsibilities and powers. As we note in our Chapter on Hazardous Wastes, the Government rejected the Royal Commission on Environmental Pollution's strong recommendation that HMIP should enjoy statutory enforcement powers over waste disposal authorities. Discharges to water from non-scheduled sites and processes are controlled not by HMIP, but by the National Rivers Authority (NRA), unless the discharge contains 'Red List' substances. In this case, HMIP will have responsibility, though the NRA will be consulted when applications to discharge are considered by HMIP. The Ministry of Agriculture, Fisheries and Food oversees sea dumping.

Although mentioned in the White Paper on the Environment, *This Common Inheritance*, the possibility of creating a more comprehensive environmental protection agency, by merging HMIP with the NRA and possibly the Health and Safety Executive, was discounted. In the Government's view, the case for this was not sufficiently strong to justify 'further administrative upheaval' for the newer organisations. However, it was proposed to consider making HMIP a separate executive agency rather than a sub-department of the DoE, and the creation of a new 'umbrella body' overseeing the NRA and HMIP was suggested for future consideration. This latter proposal suggests that the Government is beginning to consider the weaknesses of the current separation of pollution inspectorates, but prefers to tinker with add-on extras rather than attempt the much

needed re-organisation of the more fundamental struc-
tures.

Moreover, it is not yet certain whether criteria for
scheduling sites will be strict enough, or whether discharge
conditions will impose suffiiciently tough conditions. The
'Red List' as it stands is certainly inadequate; it should
include all dangerous substances that threaten human
health or the environment. There is also uncertainty about
just how much information will be available to the public.

## *Friends of the Earth Policy Recommendations*
## Pollution Control

**1.** Her Majesty's Inspectorate of Pollution must be
given the necessary financial and personnel resources
to fully implement and enforce Integrated Pollution
Control (IPC).

**2.** Applications for IPC authorisations should include environmental assessments of the options for
waste disposal. The assessments should include
energy audits and re-use possibilities.

**3.** An Environmental Protection Agency should be
established as part of an Environmental Protection
Commission with a broad remit for research, monitoring, setting quality and performance standards, enforcement and advice on all matters relating to
environmental protection.

# Chapter 8

# HAZARDOUS WASTES

The transport and disposal of wastes in Britain involves risks to both public health and the wider environment. Unfortunately there are major flaws in the waste management regime with inadequate laws, insufficient monitoring, ineffective enforcement and derisory penalties all leading to a system open to abuse.

Despite a succession of damning reports by several authoritative bodies through the last decade, the Government has, on the whole, steadfastly rejected many of the recommendations designed to remedy these deficiencies.

From time to time, public disquiet is heightened by headline news stories. In the summer of 1988, the Karin B attempted to land at a British port with a cargo of over 2,000 tonnes of toxic waste. This had originally been shipped with forged documents from Italy to Nigeria, and dumped, some of it leaking from corroding drums, in the outskirts of the port of Koko – for £60 a month rent. The Nigerian Government invited a team of toxic waste experts, including representation from Friends of the Earth, to investigate, following which the Italian Government arranged for the waste to be returned to Italy. The ship, however, was diverted to the UK. At least one UK company was quite keen to handle the waste. After a concerted campaign by Friends of the Earth, which generated considerable publicity and led to an enormous public outcry, the Karin B was eventually turned away, on the grounds that her load was not adequately documented. This whole saga high-lighted Britain's failure to implement European Community rules controlling the international movement of hazardous waste, as well as drawing attention to Britain's role as a waste dumping ground – a role which dramatically increased through the 1980s.

Hazardous chemical wastes were in the news again when protesters in Rhymney, South Wales, complained to councillors about the location of a transfer site providing temporary storage for used solvents from ink, metal cleaning and paint processes. A licence had been granted for operations to begin on a site 'within yards of the comprehensive school and the community hospital' (*Sunday Correspondent*, April 24th 1990). Labels on drums showed that the chemicals stored included methyl-ethyl-ketone (highly flammable and potentially explosive; the vapour can cause blindness and death) and tetra-chloro-ethylene (which is poisonous, can cause blindness and may cause cancer and birth defects).

Local GP Dr Ieuan Evans commented: 'I fail to see why anyone could think this is a suitable site to store dangerous chemicals.'

The local council ordered the company involved to reduce its stockpile from 7,000 to 1,000 drums and tried to revoke the licence. The company has appealed against this revocation and has challenged both the reduction in the quantities and a 28 day limit on storage imposed by the council. While the Welsh Office considers the appeal, the company can continue to ignore the proposed new licence conditions.

Rubber tyres can release a deadly cocktail of carcinogenic and toxic organic compounds when burned. In a letter to the *Guardian* of May 1st 1990, the Director of the Clyde River Purification Board recalled a 1978 fire in which 15,000 tonnes of tyres burning in an old quarry in Ayrshire 'produced an estimated 90,000 litres of black oil much of which found its way into the Dusk Water killing all fish life and most of the bottom fauna for a distance of 10 kilometres.' The letter went on to describe how workers attempting to clean up the river were provided, on the advice of the Health and Safety Executive, with impervious suits and breathing masks.

This letter was published to refute claims recently made by the Deputy Chief Executive of Powys County Council that there was no pollution risk from the burning of a 'vast dump of motor vehicle tyres'.

There are an estimated 20–30 tyre dumps in the UK, each containing over 20,000 tonnes of stockpiled tyres, many of them close to major roads and population centres. Despite the huge problem of tyre disposal, the Environment White Paper of September 1990 went no further than to state that the Government are 'considering the options'. While noting that one option would be to levy a sales tax on tyres to fund research, the Government stopped short of putting its supposed commitment to the 'Polluter Pays Principle' into practice.

The problems of leaky waste tips (many of them now closed) hit the headlines in February 1990. Friends of the Earth, in conjunction with *The Observer*, published the results of a 1974 Government study that showed that in 1300 landfill sites there was a risk that polluting effluents might leak into surface or underground water (aquifers). This is of particular concern since aquifers are a source of over a quarter of the drinking water in Britain, with this rising up to three quarters in parts of the south east.

These incidents all highlight the Government's failure, despite many warnings, to deal with all the problems of hazardous waste. Under the present system, concerns for human health and the environment all too often come a very poor second to strictly commercial considerations. Waste disposal frequently follows the line of least resistance, legal or otherwise, taking the cheapest available option.

# Legal and political responsibility

Prior to the Environmental Protection Act 1990, the responsibility for waste management rested with the Waste Disposal Authorities (WDAs), either County, District or Metropolitan Councils depending on the area. The WDAs issued licences to waste site operators, who were private companies or council bodies. Many reports have referred to the wide variation in standards of site operation and enforcement.

Hazardous waste disposal was the subject of an investigation by the House of Lords Committee on Science and Technology in 1980/81. The Committee's report noted that control by waste disposal authorities was 'defective and urgently in need of strengthening'. Several witnesses told the Committee that district councils were 'too small a unit to be effective', and the Committee recommended both the establishment of a small Hazardous Waste Inspectorate (HWI) and the formal regionalisation of disposal authorities. The HWI was formed in 1984 but regionally based disposal authorities have yet to be formed, despite the continuing inability of some authorities to properly enforce the necessary standards.

In 1985, the Hazardous Waste Inspectorate, in its first report, declared that 'all too many major hazardous waste landfill sites . . . exude an atmosphere of total dereliction and decay, are under-equipped, under-manned and operate with a notable lack of professionalism.' Its second (1986) report was entitled *'Hazardous Waste Management: ". . . Ramshackle and Antediluvian"?'*.

Its third report (1986/87) again stated that 'in some areas the voluntary arrangements are not working well', and reminded the Government of its legal duty 'to impose a statutory solution' if voluntary arrangements were unsatisfactory.

In 1987, the Hazardous Waste Inspectorate was merged

into Her Majesty's Inspectorate of Pollution (HMIP). Their first annual report, 1987/88, restated their 'concern to see higher standards of professionalism in waste disposal'. Six inspectors visited 244 sites – out of over 5,000 licensed sites.

Other bodies have expressed similar anxieties. In 1989, the House of Commons Environment Committee, looking at toxic waste disposal, commented 'allowing unscrupulous operators to dump waste almost unchecked . . . may be building up a legacy of environmental disasters for the future.' In the same year, the House of Lords Committee on Science and Technology also looked at waste disposal. They reported that 'control of waste disposal by local authorities has not been good enough'.

Many of the deficiencies in the system were exposed in evidence given by the Department of the Environment (DoE) itself to the 1989 House of Commons Environment Committee. The DoE admitted that only 23 of the 79 waste disposal Authorities in England had completed the waste disposal plans required by a section of the Control of Pollution Act 1974 which had been brought into force in 1978, some 11 years earlier. By early 1990 some 15 authorities had still failed to produce plans.

There are also no reliable statistics on waste generation and disposal in Britain. This issue was elaborated on in the first Annual Report of Her Majesty's Inspectorate of Pollution (1987/88) which stated that some WDAs' records were kept in 'the shoe box in the corner'.

The evidence also revealed the lack of resources at HMIP, which adversely affected their ability to monitor and advise. At the time, there were just five Principal Inspectors and one Chief Inspector. Whilst there have been modest staff increases since, the Inspectorate is still understaffed.

The Department of the Environment admitted that landfill charges rarely rise above £5.00 per tonne and are sometimes as low as £1.50 per tonne. This contrasts with HMIP estimates that the charges necessary in order to finance proper engineering, maintenance, restoration and aftercare would be around £9.00/tonne (1987 prices). The inescapable conclusion is that environmentally essential work is being skimped or left undone – a very serious matter given the problems that can arise in landfilling waste.

One improvement introduced under the Environmental Protection Act is the separation of councils' roles as both regulator and site operator (poacher and gamekeeper again). Arm's length companies will have to be established. Another addition to the Act has finally given powers to the Secretary of State to impose statutory regional waste authorities. However, the signs are that these powers are viewed only as a last resort. 'We do not want to use these powers, but if we must we will', said Junior Environment Minister David Heathcoat-Amory.

# Imports of waste into the UK

Britain, Government Minister Lord Belstead insisted in July 1987, deals with waste 'much better than it is dealt with elsewhere'. High standards in the UK, claims the Government, make it unnecessary to curb or effectively regulate the trade in waste imports.

The truth, unfortunately, is exactly the reverse. It is just because our standards are low and our charges correspondingly cheap that overseas waste authorities and disposal companies are keen to dump here. On the continent – especially in France, Belgium, West Germany and the Netherlands – landfilling controls were tightened during the eighties. The volume of waste imported into the UK swelled dramatically during this period. The overall figure for hazardous waste rose from around 5,000 tonnes annually in the early 1980s to over 40,000 tonnes in 1989.

The figures underestimate the real extent of the import-ation, since the present system only records so-called 'special wastes'. Such wastes are rather arbitrarily defined by reference to their potential for spontaneous combustion or certain effects on human health or prescription medicines. No explicit account is taken of the potential impact of the waste on the wider environment. Notification of other types of waste is not necessary, although recent figures from HMIP estimated that more than 130,000 tonnes of 'non-special' waste for immediate landfill would be imported in 1988/89.

In addition, it emerged in a House of Commons debate in March 1988 that even the figures for 'special waste' represent no more than 'best estimates'. HMIP have commented that 'complete figures for special wastes are difficult to obtain because of the inadequate information supplied by some Waste Disposal Authorities' and that 'several Waste Disposal Authorities have found it im-possible to provide any figures at all'.

# Landfill sites

Landfill (the dumping of waste into holes in the ground, including disused quarries, or the creation of 'waste hills') is the most common disposal method in Britain. In addition to the 4,000 currently-licensed sites operating in England and Wales, there are many thousands more closed sites (some closed before licensing was required). For many of these closed sites, virtually nothing is known about either the design and operation of the landfill or the types and quantities of the waste.

There are major problems associated with this disposal method. The liquid generated within landfills, leachate, can be highly toxic. It can seep out, polluting both surface and groundwater.

The decomposing waste matter can also produce danger-ous cóncentrations of explosive methane gas. At Loscoe, in Derbyshire, three people were seriously injured in March 1986 when a pocket of gas from a domestic and commercial waste tip exploded in a bungalow 25 yards from the site boundary. The tip had been closed four years previously.

In December 1987, HMIP and the Waste Disposal Authorities surveyed landfill gas hazards. However, they omitted sites closed prior to 1977 to make the task 'manageable'. Even so, some 1,300 sites posed a potential hazard from methane generation. The location of these sites has not been disclosed. The risks from migrating gas can only be reduced by constant monitoring and gas migration controls. In the 600 or so cases where there are buildings nearby (mostly within 100 metres), additional gas migration controls are estimated to cost £250 million.

In the two years to 1989, 20 explosions or near misses were recorded in a sample of less than one-fifth of the counties of England. In this context, the £33 million mentioned in the White Paper on the Environment for remedial work at landfill sites appears a feeble sum.

The problems posed by leachate were outlined in a Department of the Environment report in 1988:

> Landfill sites are a major threat to groundwater quality and a number of cases of pollution attributable to landfill are recorded. . . . All Water Authorities report ground-water pollution problems with landfill sites to a varying degree, and in many cases it is regarded as the most significant threat.

A recent Government-commissioned report carried out by the Environmental Safety Centre at Harwell was published in May 1990. This study of 100 major landfill sites (accounting for over half of waste going to landfill in Britain) revealed widespread problems. No monitoring for water pollution was undertaken at one third of sites. Where monitoring was carried out, some pollution of water was measured in over half the sites, and in the majority of these cases no action had been taken to control the problem. Similarly, a third of sites had no monitoring for gas migration problems, over half of the others had detectable gas migration, and no action had been taken at a third of these sites. The report also showed that few sites met the Government's recommendations for permeability, many made no attempt to control smells, birds or dust and many had no arrangements for properly examining the types or quantities of waste accepted. The report concluded that these deficiencies negated any efforts to improve standards of landfill sites in recent years. Moreover, the authors went so far as to admit that the report probably underestimated the problem since the survey was biased towards the new, presumably better-run sites.

Following Friends of the Earth's Toxic Tips Campaign in February 1990, the Environment Minister, David Trippier, commented that 'extensive controls ensure that sites are properly managed and safeguarded against pollution'. However, in the September 1990 White Paper, the Government recognised that there may have been 'some pollution' from landfall sites, although in 'relatively few' instances. This is simply not supported by the facts.

# Pressure from the European Commission

As in so many environmental matters, Britain has obstinately resisted growing pressure to adopt the standards proposed by our European partners on the shipment and disposal of dangerous wastes.

In June 1988, Community Environment Ministers

proposed a ban on waste shipments from the EEC to Third World countries. Britain opposed the ban.

In September 1988, after threats of legal action from the Commission, Britain moved tardily to comply with two Directives on the transfrontier shipment of hazardous wastes. In the case of the first, covering intra-EC shipments, we were three years late; in the case of the second, which regulated exports to the Third World, we were almost two years late.

The British response was devious as well as belated. A loophole was created by adopting the very limited British criteria for 'special wastes' – which fails to pay explicit heed to environmental as well as human health hazards – to define hazardous waste. The Government may well be contravening the 1978 Directive on toxic and dangerous wastes, which defines such wastes at those which threaten human health and/or the environment. It certainly seems intent on trying to define some of the problems out of existence rather than actually tackling all of them.

Forthcoming legislation from the European Commission – assuming it is implemented, monitored and enforced – should mean improvements in waste management in this country. Measures proposed would improve landfilling standards, give producers of waste strict 'no-fault' liability for any problems caused by the waste generated (until the final disposal), increase freedom of information and access to monitoring data and provide more thorough definitions of waste and hazardous waste.

# Government action and continuing problems

Despite some decidedly modest moves of late in the Environmental Protection Act, mainly in response to growing public disquiet and the manifest crisis of the system, the Government's overall record on the problem of waste management and disposal is inglorious. Fundamental concerns about lack of resources and expertise have not been challenged.

The Environmental Protection Act separates the regulatory and operational (gamekeeper and poacher!) functions of the Waste Disposal Authorities, so creating Waste Regulatory Authorities and local authority-owned waste disposal companies. Also new is the 'duty of care' imposed on all those involved in the waste chain from producer to final disposer. However, the accompanying draft Code of Conduct is a minefield of imprecise terms and may encourage some waste producers to do even less than at present. This change is far weaker than the European Commission's proposed Directive on civil liability for pollution by waste.

A further limited change will prevent the holder of a disposal licence from relinquishing, at any time, the licence and thereby walking away from any responsibility to undertake further additional environmental controls. The proposed change will require the regulatory authority to issue a certificate of completion only when it is satisfied that the site poses no threat of pollution. However, the extent of the evidence to be submitted by the licence holder and the criteria for accepting the surrender of the licence have yet to be specified.

The Environmental Protection Act also imposes new responsibilities for old, closed landfill sites. Clean-up of any problem sites becomes a 'duty' of the relevant Waste Regulatory Authority.

As yet, however, the Government's record remains undistinguished. We have already noted its failure to implement many of the recommendations of a series of expert reports through the 1980s. We have also mentioned the work of the House of Lords Committee on Science and

Technology, which in 1981 published the results of its inquiry into hazardous waste disposal. It took the Government some six and a half years to respond to this report. And the response? The extra controls proposed on undeclared wastes were rejected as unnecessary – and so was the suggestion that waste imports should be pre-notified. Yet in December 1981, the Government had promised the House of Commons no less than three times that these matters would be regulated at the earliest opportunity.

During the 1980s, two waste management consultation papers were issued. But both were shelved, and for several years neither new legislation nor new regulations were introduced.

Lack of resources is a recurrent theme. In October 1988, HMIP issued a revised edition of a 1976 Waste Management Paper. This tightened controls over site licensing, enforcement of licence conditions, and site inspection. But in the absence of the necessary additional resources this could prove a dead letter. In September 1988, the Royal Commission on Environmental Pollution urged the Government to increase HMIP's funding, and to give it statutory powers of enforcement over the waste disposal authorities. Currently HMIP's role is merely to oversee the operations of WDAs. Rejecting this appeal, Lord Caithness said that the proposal would change HMIP's role 'very radically'.

In our view, such radical change is precisely what is required. HMIP needs more clout.

*Friends of the Earth Policy Recommendations*
# Hazardous Wastes

**1.** The Government should promote an integrated approach to waste management. This should cover raw materials, the manufacturing processes and the design and use of products. Priority should be given to the operation and design of processes and products to facilitate the reclamation of materials and minimise waste.

**2.** Producers of waste should have an absolute and retrospective liability, with a 'cradle to grave' responsibility for all wastes produced and any problems it may cause.

**3.** A fund should be established to pay for the clean-up costs of contaminated land where the waste producer cannot be identified or is clearly unable to foot the bill. This should be financed by green taxes on waste producers.

**4.** Regional waste regulatory authorities should be established under the control of an Environmental Protection Commission.

**5.** Consignment notes and certified analytical results detailing contents, origin and destination for all wastes (other than genuinely inert ones) and not just 'special wastes', should be required.

**6.** All producers of waste, waste disposers and Waste Regulatory Authorities should maintain public registers containing detailed information about the nature and quantities of waste generated, transported and disposed.

**7.** The Government should support bans on all transboundary shipments of wastes both between EEC member states and between the EEC and other countries.

# Chapter 9

# BEYOND THE BOTTLE BANK: RECYCLING

Shortage of landfill space, problems of water contamination from waste sites, air pollution from burning rubbish, the squandering of valuable resources involved in our throw-away lifestyle – there are many good reasons for promoting recycling and reuse. Environment Secretary Chris Patten recognised this when he told the 1989 Conservative Party Conference: 'We should aim to recycle half our household waste within ten years.' Excellent news: Britain would move up, at last, from near the bottom of the western European recycling league. For once, we would really be able to claim to be taking an environmental lead.

However, Chris Patten's clear commitment has been modified, and the Government now wants to recycle half our 'potentially recyclable' domestic waste.

A cynic might conclude that all that is actually being recycled is green rhetoric, and that nothing much is going to change.

That would be a pity, because the record hitherto is very poor. And the opportunities are great.

# Britain's Record

West Germany claims to recycle 20 per cent of its domestic waste – a proportion ten times greater than we achieve here. Friends of the Earth's analysis of the Government's own figures shows that between 55 and 60 per cent of our rubbish could be recycled, even without any advances in technology. At the moment, we recycle less than two per cent.

In Britain, just 300,000 tonnes of glass, only 17 per cent of consumption, was recycled in 1989. Several other countries, such as the Netherlands, manage over 50 per cent already, and European countries as a whole (EC countries, Austria and Switzerland) averaged twice the British figure, 33 per cent, during 1988.

Collection and recycling of other materials is similarly poor. Aluminium in cans is consumed at the rate of 40,000 tonnes annually, and of this approximately ten per cent is recovered. Only about eight per cent of steel cans were recycled here in 1989, while West Germany recycled 40 per cent and the Netherlands 45 per cent. The Warren Spring Laboratory Recycling Advisory Unit, set up by the Government in 1986, estimates that 10 million tonnes of paper and board products are used each year in Britain. Of this, just under 9 million tonnes could be recovered. But the actual recovery rate is only 28 per cent.

One scheme at least in Britain is achieving substantially more than the national average. In Stocksbridge, Sheffield, the country's first 'blue box' or door-to-door collection scheme was launched by Friends of the Earth in November 1989. Within just six months, it was collecting over 20 per cent of Stocksbridge's waste.

Although the Stocksbridge scheme is the first in the UK, there are door-to-door collection schemes in more and more North American states. Householders separate their waste into different bins – the blue boxes – and these are collected in a compartmentalised lorry, and sent for recycling. The introduction of widespread door-to-door collection of this kind would be necessary if Britain was seriously to aim at increasing the proportion of waste recycled from its current paltry level of two per cent.

Blue box collections in Canada have been greatly helped by the three-way funding they receive from local authorities, central government, and the industries which produce the waste in the first place.

In Britain, the Government has been emphatic in refusing local authorities any more funding to set up separate recycling collections. 'It would be wrong to subsidise the collection and recycling of waste in this way,' said Heathcoat-Amory, Junior Environment Minister, in a written answer to a House of Commons question of 5 March 1990. The denial of the funding and help which is clearly needed gives the Government's boasts of commitment to domestic waste recycling a distinctly hollow ring.

Recycling does the community a greater service than regular waste disposal by averting potential environmental damage and conserving resources, yet these advantages yield no financial profits. For example, recycling batteries is expensive, and extremely unlikely to pay for itself without government intervention. However, it is very important, since potentially poisonous metals such as cadmium and lead otherwise contaminate landfill sites and could eventually pollute groundwater.

The waste of organic matter provides another good example of the need for coordinated efforts and funding at local authority level. Organic waste – food, garden material, even newspapers (which were once trees) – rotting in landfill sites produces landfill gas. This potent mix includes methane, which is highly explosive. It is also one of the greenhouse gases, contributing to global warming.

For those two compelling reasons, the organic part of

domestic waste should be recycled. But there is no industry responsible for producing it, as there is for a can or a newspaper. No voluntary group would be willing to collect organic waste for fundraising, and you can't put a deposit on a potato to get its peel back. Not everyone has a garden, and so not everyone can start their own compost heap, but everyone throws organic waste away.

The only way to ensure that organic waste gets recycled on a large scale is for local authorities to set up schemes, with or without private sector involvement, to compost the organic fraction of our waste. Compost made from domestic waste could provide valuable soil conditioner and nutrients, and could help reduce demand for peat, protecting peat bogs which are being destroyed at an alarming rate.

This requires capital spending, which is becoming increasingly difficult for local authorities wary of increasing their spending and perhaps incurring poll tax caps. So government money, or help in finding money, is essential. Legislation to encourage local authorities to help voluntary groups allows the Government to claim it is encouraging recycling, but this merely shifts responsibility in a meaningless way unless more financial help, or at least the opportunity to raise money, is given.

# EC Directive

A European Directive on Containers of Liquids for Human Consumption was adopted in 1985. It asked Member States to take steps to reduce the environmental impact of drinks packaging, although no targets or arrangements are specified.

Britain's response to the Directive stressed once again the 'voluntary approach', and neither regulation nor enforcement were introduced in the UK. In consequence, the impact of the Directive here has been very limited.

The packaging industry, in a series of voluntary agreements, said that it would continue its policy of 'lightweighting' – using less material to make the same sized container – which is a cost-cutting measure anyway. The finite limits to reducing the amount of material in any container mean that lightweighting can achieve only a limited reduction in waste. In practice, lightweighting is no substitute for recycling or re-use policies.

One of the Government's few concrete commitments was to increase bottle banks to provide one for every 10,000 people by 1991. But even this solid commitment is far too weak – Austria already has one bottle bank for every 1,200 people, France and Germany both have one for every 2,000, and the Netherlands has one for every 1,400 people. The Netherlands recycles over 60 per cent of its glass.

The Government showed itself very keen to avoid putting too much of a burden on industry when meeting the Directive. It has showed the same attitude when discussing the proposed amendment to the Directive, which suggested that countries introduce targets for recycling and/or re-use rates, and mandatory labels. In a letter to the European Commission, the Department of Trade and Industry spoke of the 'general unease about the threat of adding a further legal requirement for packaging . . . The UK government is committed to a policy of deregulation.'

There has been some progress since the Directive was introduced, but this is due more to the threat of more demanding European legislation than to the voluntary agreements made under the terms of the existing Directive.

Refillable bottles, provided enough of them are refilled, are the most resource and energy efficient way of packaging drinks. If milk bottles were replaced with one-trip paper cartons, an extra 57,000 tonnes of waste would be produced each year. The Waste Management Advisory Council recommended in 1981 that systems for 'refillables' should be improved, but this has still not been backed by Government action.

For instance, publicity and promotion of refillables are clearly needed. Quite simply, people do not know where to take their refillable bottles, or even whether a particular bottle is refillable. According to the packaging industry itself, £7.5 million of deposits on bottles remains unclaimed each year.

Can recovery banks are thin on the ground. There were just 217 sites in the Save-a-Can scheme at the end of May 1990. British Steel recently bought the Save-a-Can scheme, and has expanded its target to 1,000 banks by 1994. This would still only be one for every 56,000 people. Magnetic extraction of cans from mixed rubbish also takes place in 26 places in the UK. In all, about eight per cent of steel cans were recycled in 1989. Aluminium cans are also recovered through schemes encouraged by the Aluminium Can Recycling Association, set up in 1989.

Other industries are doing little or nothing. Belatedly, the plastics industry is now beginning to consider post-consumer recycling schemes, but this has more to do with fears of impending European legislation, expected to set recycling targets, than UK Government action. A new company called Recoup has been formed with support from 25 plastic container firms to promote plastic bottle recycling – 'after earlier attempts to head off the issue'. By anticipating and meeting European targets for plastic recycling voluntarily, the industry hopes to avoid 'packaging taxes, deposits or some other onerous and logistical burden'. Working with other interested groups, Recoup have so far helped organise collection schemes in Milton Keynes and Leeds.

Another particularly depressing revelation of the Government's real attitude came in 1988, when Britain joined the European Commission in taking proceedings against Denmark to the European Court of Justice.

The Danes require all beer, soft drinks and mineral waters to be sold in standard returnable bottles, with a deposit and collection system for non-standard bottles. Metal cans are banned. The scheme has been extremely successful, with 99 per cent of standard bottles returned and refilled.

The Commission, backed by the UK, argued that this represented an 'excessive level of environmental protection', and infringed the Treaty of Rome's provisions of free trade. However, the Court supported the Danes and threw out the Commission's case. In a judgement of historic importance, it ruled that 'protection of the environment constitutes an imperative requirement', and as such can lawfully limit the application of free trade rules. Neither industry nor governments can now oppose can bans or mandatory deposit schemes as being illegal under European law.

Despite this sorry episode, the British Government has taken some welcome recycling initiatives. The establishment of the Recycling Advisory Unit at the Warren Spring Laboratory was a step forward. However, Government initiatives have not always produced results. The appointment of a Minister with responsibility for recycling in the Department of Trade and Industry had limited effect. Problems have arisen because responsibility for waste and recycling is fragmented between two Departments. Environment has the main responsibility for the collection of waste and so for recyclable materials, while Trade and Industry is responsible for markets and end-uses of materials.

# Markets

Collecting waste for recycling is only half the story. If no-one uses that waste to make new products, it will not have been recycled, and the environmental benefits associated with recycling will not happen. All that will have been achieved is a glorified rubbish collection.

The Government-backed Regional Waste Paper Seminars of 1989 did not recognise this and were badly mistimed. Despite warnings from Friends of the Earth and waste paper merchants, the seminars encouraged the collection of low grade waste paper just as the market went into surplus. The over-supply of low grade paper, such as newspapers, caused the price for used newspapers to collapse from its 1988 level of around £25 a tonne. Currently (September 1990) waste paper merchants pay nothing to voluntary groups for low grade paper collection. Hundreds of small community schemes have crumpled. This under-lines the need to encourage the use of recycled paper, as well as backing collection schemes.

Here again, legislation is crucial. California, and some other US states, have legislated that newspapers must use 25 per cent recycled fibre by 1991, and 50 per cent by 2000. In another move, all US State and Federal institutions now have to use recycled paper. As well as guaranteeing a market for waste, these moves will spur more US and Canadian paper companies to invest in the equipment necessary to convert waste paper into new paper. Commit-ments to using higher proportions of recycled fibre by newspaper publishers here would similarly stimulate the market for used newspapers.

Friends of the Earth has called on the Government to introduce similar legislation, requiring all tiers of govern-ment to buy recycled paper, but it has refused to legislate on this matter.

In March 1990, government advisors recommended that VAT on products made of certain recycled materials should be zero-rated, but when a junior Treasury minister, Mr Ryder, was asked in the House of Commons whether this would happen, he replied with a simple 'No'.

The Government has been regrettably, if characteristic-ally, reluctant to use direction and enforcement. As ever, it seeks 'voluntary agreement' – a recipe for inaction if agreement is not reached. Mounting seminars and producing videos (such as 'Watch Your Waste', made by the Recycling Advisory Unit in 1987, which advised industry on how to produce less waste) may be useful educational exercises, but they are no substitute for legal regulation. The Government, as we shall see, has provided some financial backing for voluntary collection schemes. However, these can never be an alternative to the comprehensive, integrated approach we need, which would bring in regulations to reduce waste as well as to encourage its recycling.

# Voluntary and community schemes

Giving financial help to voluntary groups has been the Government's main way of supporting recycling. UK 2000, a government-funded organisation set up to encourage practical environmental projects, has given grants to Friends of the Earth, primarily for recycling work. The 'Waste Watch' campaign organised by the National Council for Voluntary Organisations, which encourages recycling by voluntary groups, is part-funded by the Government. Both the Department of the Environment and the Department of Trade and Industry have helped support Recycling City, a major Friends of the Earth project set up in 1989 to provide examples of good recycling practice. Sheffield became the first city in the project, joined by Cardiff in May 1990. Dundee will soon become the third Recycling City, and one other location has yet to be decided. Sheffield and Cardiff both run door-to-door collections of recyclable waste. Up to now, the Government's contribution to Recycling City is, in total, somewhere in the region of £150,000, just over half the amount provided by the major corporate sponsor of the project, British Telecom.

Small scale projects have provided useful income for a range of organisations, from the Boy Scouts to the many local Friends of the Earth groups which run collections or staff skips once a month. People welcome the opportunity to use such recycling schemes. However, valued as they are by both voluntary groups and local communities, these schemes can make little impact on a national scale. Recycling would be better served by more comprehensive schemes, ensuring continuity of labour, better geographical coverage and co-ordination, efficiencies of scale, and strategic planning.

# Local authorities

The Government provides no incentives to local authorities to set up recycling schemes. All the same, some extensive and popular projects have been launched and are setting an example of what can be achieved. Socially and geographically diverse, Leeds and Richmond nonetheless have one thing in common: both communities recycle a growing proportion of their waste.

Leeds SWAP (Save Waste and Prosper) collects waste at 131 sites in the city, and is setting up a door-to-door collection scheme. Richmond has sixteen sites, not just for cans, paper and bottles, but also for textiles and oil. Both schemes return profits to the community by way of local charities.

In 1987, Richmond extracted 2,800 tonnes of waste for recycling – waste that would otherwise have been a financial as well as environmental burden. A growing number of local councils now offer rebates to voluntary groups that collect waste for recycling, but these rarely if ever reflect the true savings made by the councils. This will be partially rectified by the Environmental Protection Act.

# The Environmental Protection Act

Ministers have claimed that the Environmental Protection Act will bring major advances for recycling. During Parliamentary debate on the Bill, it was stated that it would 'help to bring recycling to the forefront of waste disposal strategies in the United Kingdom' (Heathcoat-Amory, April 25th 1990). In fact the Environmental Protection Act will do little to increase recycling, and nothing to increase re-use.

Local authorities will be obliged to write plans for recycling, but these plans are not legally enforceable. Amendments to the Bill proposed obligatory duties to implement recycling plans, but these were rejected by the Government.

Following pressure from Friends of the Earth, the Government included one important amendment in the Bill. Waste disposal authorities will be obliged to reflect savings in disposal costs and pay waste collectors who reduce the amount of waste needing disposal by diverting it to recycling schemes. However, savings in collection costs will not be similarly passed on to voluntary groups or businesses which save work for the collection authorities.

The Act may make it easier for those authorities committed to recycling, but it provides no incentive for those many authorities which remain apathetic.

# The White Paper

In early 1990, a series of Advisory Groups were set up to advise the Government on the recycling section of the White Paper.

The Government declined to publish their recommendations. These included tax breaks for capital spending on recycling equipment, tax reductions for products containing recycled materials, regulations for recycling rates for certain materials, taxes on items that cause problems in the waste stream, and further measures to increase the use of refillable bottles.

In fact, the White Paper on the Environment, published in September 1990, contained little more than commitments repeated from the Environmental Protection Act, and items for 'further discussion and voluntary action'.

There were only two new announcements – two research projects on the recycling of construction waste, and a requirement on local authorities to 'take account of' recycling facilities when assessing planning applications for 'large' shopping developments. This requirement was not accompanied by a timetable, and the terms 'to take account of' and 'large' were not explained or defined.

Advice from the Recycling Advisory Groups was largely ignored. Those recommendations which were referred to in the White Paper, such as taxes on items which are a problem in the waste stream, will be 'discussed' and 'studied' rather than implemented.

What is missing is a timetabled programme for action. Chris Patten will have to produce one soon if he really wants to meet his recycling target.

*Friends of the Earth Policy Recommendations*
# Recycling

1. The Government's commitment to recycling must be extended beyond domestic waste to the other 96 per cent of the waste stream. As a first step, the Government must commit itself to recycling 50 per

cent of *all* domestic waste (not 50 per cent of the 'recyclable' fraction) by the year 2000.

**2.**   All households and commercial premises currently served by a waste collection service should also be served by a recycling collection. This does not negate the need for communal recycling collection facilities in some areas.

**3.**   Recycling collections should be run as a public service, although this does not rule out services being contracted out to private companies.

**4.**   Markets for recycled materials should be regulated, to avoid wide fluctuations in the market price for such materials.

**5.**   The Government should create markets and stimulate demand for reclaimed materials through measures including setting minimum standards for content of recycled materials in goods and obligatory preferential purchase of recycled materials by public bodies and by specific sectors of industry.

**6.**   Fiscal and other measures should be introduced to encourage industry to increase its commitment to recycling. Tax relief should be provided for the capital costs of recycling plant.

**7.**   The re-use of containers should be maximised through mandatory standardisation of designs and financial incentives.

**8.**   Government should provide incentives for all waste producers to minimise waste output.

# Chapter 10

# ECO-LABELLING OR GREEN CONS?

A walk round any supermarket will confirm the influence of the 'green consumer'. Phosphate-free washing powders, organic vegetables, ozone-friendly aerosols and a variety of other products, proclaiming ecological benefits, line the shelves to tempt the environmentally concerned shopper.

Unfortunately, things are not as straightforward as they might at first seem. The plethora of green logos, which usually suggest some unspecified benefit to the environment, often confuse rather than inform. And many of the claims made are quite misleading.

## 'Environmentally friendly'?

Such slogans as 'environmentally friendly' are widely used. One manufacturer has suggested, for instance, that once chlorofluorocarbons (CFCs) are removed, aerosols inflict no damage on the environment. The claim is absurd. Aerosols take energy to manufacture, and because so many aerosols are potentially explosive, people should not be inadvertently encouraged to 'wash and squash' them to recycle them through can banks. Many of them use damaging chemicals other than CFCs. Some aerosols have even been labelled 'ozone-friendly' when they have contained ozone-depleting chemicals such as 1,1,1,-trichloroethane (also known as methyl chloroform).

More generally, it is worth pointing out that every product has some environmental impact, even if only through the energy used in its manufacture and transportation.

The confusion, and deliberate misinformation, involved in so much green marketing was the target of Friends of the Earth's 'Green Con of the Year' Award in 1989. The intention was to embarrass companies who treated the environment as a marketing ploy and to encourage them, if they were genuinely concerned, to review the environmental impact of all their activities. The Award also highlighted the need for legislation to control misleading environmental claims in product advertising and merchandising.

The results were announced in December 1989. Overall winners were British Nuclear Fuels, whose attempt to portray nuclear power as clean and green was described by Jonathon Porritt as 'the ultimate green con'. Runners up, Higgs Furs, marketed fox furs as 'environmentally friendly'. There were also special section awards for the aerosol and motor industries. Friends of the Earth has decided to make this an annual event until there ceases to be a need for it.

Meanwhile, general public concern about the situation was becoming evident. Following the initial surge of enthusiasm, scepticism about 'green products' was understandably setting in. Many people, however, continued to respond to green slogans and logos under the mistaken impression that they reflected official approval of some kind. A *Which?* survey of September 1989 found that over half those questioned, shown a typically 'environmentally friendly' label, thought it met some set of independent standards. Of these people, 44 per cent thought the labels were actually approved by the Government. (In fact it is, of course, manufacturers themselves who apply these 'green labels' to their products.) Of those who correctly stated that no official approval was implied by such labels, 83 per cent thought that such approval should be required.

The need for government action to bring forward an official labelling scheme was becoming clear, even though as late as April 1989 Trade and Industry Minister Tony Newton was telling the CBI conference 'Green Consumer – Green Business' that he, and the Government, preferred if possible to sustain 'the voluntary approach'. In August 1989, however, a Government discussion paper signalling the intention to introduce an official scheme was published. Criticisms of this paper ('Environmental Labelling – A Discussion Paper'), which many saw as weak and half-hearted, led to a revised set of proposals being announced by Environment Secretary Chris Patten in January 1990.

# Proposals for an official scheme

Official environmental labelling schemes are not a new idea. West Germany had one as early as 1978, and they exist in other countries such as Canada and Japan. Their common basic idea is that an official logo is awarded to products less environmentally damaging than their competitors. Shoppers can make an informed choice secure in the knowledge that they are not being conned and that the product has been officially assessed. Businesses have a marketing incentive (providing the qualification criteria are suitably strict) to manufacture less environmentally damaging products so they can receive an 'EcoLogo'.

On 23 May 1990, the Government announced the formation of a panel, to be chaired by Sir Kenneth Durham, to advise on the founding and running of a similar scheme here. It is impossible to know exactly what the panel will recommend, but the British Government has been monitoring the Canadian 'Environmental Choice' scheme closely. This scheme appears to fit in with Chris Patten's thinking and it is likely that a similar model will be used in Britain.

The Canadian scheme is overseen by a sixteen-strong board, appointed by the government and composed of representatives of environmental and consumer groups and of manufacturers and retailers.

The board's first task has been to identify product categories in which considerable environmental savings can be made. To assess these potential savings, every aspect of a product's 'life cycle' is subjected to environmental impact scrutiny: raw material extraction, energy consumption, suitability for recycling, waste and disposal aspects, and so on.

Draft guidelines are then published. The public and interested bodies are given the opportunity to suggest changes and improvements. When the guidelines have been established, suppliers of products in the chosen categories can apply for the EcoLogo. In Canada, seven categories have so far been drawn up: zinc-air batteries, water-based paint, fine recycled paper, miscellaneous re-cycled paper, recycled newsprint, heat recovery ventilators and cloth nappies.

Products submitted for the EcoLogo are assessed by the Canadian Standards Association and those meeting the requirements of the scheme are licensed for three years. After that period, they will be required to re-apply: a key element of the system is regular updating of standards to take account of technological change.

# Advantages of a tiered system

In the view of Friends of the Earth, the type of scheme

likely to be introduced in this country will not be sufficiently rigorous.

Government proposals envisage companies applying for the approved label on a voluntary basis. In our view, the scheme should be compulsory, forcing all products in given categories to be assessed.

In connection with a mandatory scheme, a tiered or 'ranked' assessment would have great advantages. A product's environmental performance might be graded on a five-star rating: one star would be easily achievable and the minimum standard acceptable, five stars would be at the limit of technological capability. Naturally, assessment criteria would be reviewed and updated regularly to take account of new information and technology. Companies would then compete with each other in terms of environmental excellence, just as they do in terms of price and performance (though product performance would in fact be a factor in the awarding of an EcoLogo). Products failing to achieve even one star would have to improve or cease being offered for sale.

To date, the Government and, indeed, other countries have preferred a pass-or-fail award to a tiered scheme. The pass mark in such a system, Chris Patten has said, 'should be set towards the top end of what technology permits, but not so high as to distort the market or impose disproportionate costs on business.'

# Electrical appliances and tropical rainforests

Friends of the Earth is also campaigning for mandatory labels in areas outside the existing environmental labelling proposals. In particular, electrical appliances should be rated in terms of their energy efficiency, and tropical timber should be subject to a compulsory certification scheme.

A comprehensive, standardised scheme for the energy efficiency labelling of all electrical appliances will enable consumers to make an informed choice when buying them. This will cut domestic electricity bills and benefit the environment. At the moment, there is little sign that energy use is an issue for most purchasers. A labelling scheme can begin to raise the issue's profile and pave the way to a much more energy-conscious and energy-efficient society.

Key features of a successful scheme will include the use of standard units, allowing ready comparison between (say) fridges of different sizes. In the case of refrigerators, the standard unit would be kilowatt hours per litre volume per year. Banding or rating systems (one to five stars, or points out of ten) should give a clear message as to the energy efficiency of a given appliance in relation to all similar appliances on the market (and not just other models in the same shop or catalogue). There should be a general statement that a higher points rating means less environmental pollution is produced by the appliance and it costs less to run.

The Government's ideas on energy efficiency labelling have not changed in eleven years. Baroness Hooper, then Parliamentary Under Secretary of State for Energy, wrote to Friends of the Earth in 1989, stating that 'it has been policy since 1979 that energy labelling should be a voluntary matter for the manufacturers and retailers'.

This line has been continued in the recent White Paper on the Environment, *This Common Inheritance.* Despite the obvious opportunity to announce a labelling scheme (itself a soft option over compulsory legal targets for energy efficiency), the Government announced that they will press for an 'effective Community scheme, if possible a voluntary one'. The Government's Energy Efficiency Office has doubted the value of the voluntary approach to labels. A 1990 report stated that 'legislation to ensure compliance' was probably required.

A scheme for 'labelling' buildings in terms of their energy consumption could be adopted, and the White Paper gives some commitment to consideration of such schemes. Progress, however, will apparently have to await amendment of the Building Regulations. The UK Government vetoed a draft EC Directive on energy labelling of buildings, proposed by the European Commission in 1987. This Directive, if adopted, would have made an energy audit of buildings compulsory on change of ownership.

Friends of the Earth also calls for the introduction of a mandatory tropical timber labelling and certification scheme. In February 1990, the International Tropical Timber Organisation, with the backing of the UK Government, launched an investigation into the feasibility of a labelling scheme. In the view of Friends of the Earth, information on labels should include the country of origin, a guarantee that the timber came from a government-approved forest management plan (with provision for environmental protection), and a guarantee that production conformed to internationally agreed standards of 'best forestry management'.

Further details, and more general arguments in support of our views, will be found in the sections on Energy and on Tropical Rainforests.

# The Trades Description Act

In January 1990, the Department of Trade and Industry announced that they were considering amending the Trades Description Act. It is proposed that it should be made clear that environmental claims are trade descriptions for the purposes of the Act and that general terms such as 'environmentally friendly' fall within its scope. Consideration is also being given to whether claims should be backed with information as to their basis, and to whether claims should be treated as false unless those making them can demonstrate their truth. The advisability of introducing a new Code of Conduct is also being considered, along with whether it should be mandatory or voluntary.

While self-regulation by such organisations as the Incorporated Society of British Advertisers is welcome, such efforts have not put an end to spurious claims. Legislation is undoubtedly needed. Unfortunately, Parliamentary time may not be found. Friends of the Earth is pressing the Government to ensure that time is in fact found to debate much-needed and rigorous improvements to the Trades Description Act.

This legislation will be a useful complement to whatever labelling scheme emerges. With 1992 in view, the European Parliament is moving towards the introduction of a European-wide eco-labelling scheme. While Friends of the Earth (like Chris Patten) favours the adoption of a European system, we also believe that a British scheme, which will be quicker to prepare, should be introduced as soon as possible, preferably before the end of 1991.

Eco-labelling's contribution to a better environment depends on the continuance of the present surge of public concern about 'green issues'. But eco-labelling can also help inform and sustain that concern. For many consumers, moreover, environmental impact is still a very low priority, behind price and brand loyalty, and a labelling scheme may encourage them to rethink. Altogether, the opportunity is there for Government to take a significant step forward in lessening the impact of products on the environment. Minimium standards are essential. If a product is too wasteful of resources, too polluting, or too energy inefficient, then it should not be sold.

*Friends of the Earth Policy Recommendations*
# Eco-Labelling

**1.** The official environmental and ecological labelling of products should be compulsory for all products within designated categories. A tiered or banded system, rather than a 'pass-or-fail' system, should be used. Products failing to meet minimum criteria should be withdrawn from sale.

**2.** A compulsory energy efficiency labelling scheme for electrical appliances should allow consumers to make an informed choice of the most energy-efficient appliances. [*Reiterated as part of 'Global Warming' Policy Recommendation #1, 'Energy' Policy Recommendation #1*]

**3.** A compulsory certification and labelling scheme for tropical timber should be introduced, to ensure that imported tropical timber comes from substainably managed forests.

**4.** The Trades Description Act should be amended to bring all environmental claims clearly within its scope.

# Chapter 11

# ENVIRONMENTAL RESEARCH

In her celebrated November 1989 speech to the United Nations, helping to alert the world to the perils of global warming, Mrs Thatcher said:

> Before we act, we need the best possible scientific assessment, otherwise we risk making matters worse. We must use science to cast a light ahead, so that we can move step by step in the right direction.

This sounds like a clear signal for scientific resources to be directed at some of the major environmental problems of the world. But, all too often, the need for further evidence or scientific proof has been cited as an excuse to delay action. If the money had been forthcoming to fund the necessary research, then such statements would sound less hollow. During the 1980s, science as a whole received what the outgoing editor of New Scientist magazine (June 2nd 1990) called 'the hardest battering that British science has ever seen.'

For the fact is that Mrs Thatcher has presided over a Government that has consistently cut funding for research, including environmental studies. 'Fiscal attrition' begun in the 1970s became 'enforced decimation' of research establishments according to an editorial in Nature (March 22nd 1990). There have been small increases in the budgets of some programmes and there are signs that the worst of the cuts are now over. However, long-term damage has been done to the science base of the country. This may mean delays in the acknowledgement of problems and in remedial action.

Government funding of civil research and development (R&D) (as opposed to defence research and development) has steadily declined, both in real terms, and as a proportion of gross domestic product (GDP). In 1981, civil R&D amounted to 0.72 per cent of GDP, but this had declined to 0.55 per cent in 1988. Government plans show that total spending on civil R&D will decline by a further twelve per cent from 1989/90 to 1992/3.

The UK has also been accused of some inflation of its research and development figures, by including its support for military product development in announced figures. Almost one half (44 per cent in 1988) of the total R&D budget is spent on military and defence research and development – £2.2 billion a year in 1989/90.

The Department of Education and Science budget for science, which is distributed to the Research Councils, including the Agriculture and Food Research Council and the Natural Environment Research Council (NERC), has increased by 27 per cent in real terms in the last two years (1988/89 compared to 1990/91), but only by 28 per cent as compared with 1979/80.

# Grants, cuts and inconsistencies

Certain sectors of science involved in environmental research have fared well. In particular, money has been earmarked for UK contributions to international projects, such as the Ocean Flux Study and the World Ocean Circulation Experiment. Six million pounds has been granted towards the cost of refurbishing the research ship

*RRS Discovery*, which will gather data for global climate studies. Such studies can provide invaluable information about global climate change and the role of marine plankton in absorbing carbon dioxide from the atmosphere. Some results indicate that oceans may be absorbing less of the man-made carbon dioxide than predicted.

Also welcome was an extra £23 million grant to the British Antarctic Survey (a NERC institute), which brought the hole in the ozone layer to international attention in 1984. The money is being spent on a research ship, the *RRS James Clark Ross*, to replace the ageing *RRS John Biscoe*, and on the rebuilding of the Halley research base in Antarctica, which is being slowly crushed by accumulating snow and ice. Much of the work that led to the discovery of the depletion of the ozone layer was conducted from the Halley base. The British Geological Survey, which pessimists thought doomed, has been reprieved and given a £12 million boost.

Unfortunately, these welcome announcements have to be set against simultaneous cuts in equally valuable research. Faced with dwindling funding from the Department of Education and Science (DES), NERC has tried to protect longer-term projects which rely on a steady flow of data. Despite these efforts, NERC has been forced to announce considerable cuts. In mid-1988, for instance, 160 posts were listed by NERC for redundancies. Those to lose their jobs included researchers from the Institute of Terrestrial Ecology, who were studying population ecology of birds, bats and spiders, and 62 marine researchers at establishments such as the Plymouth Marine Laboratory and the Institute of Oceanographic Sciences Laboratory, researching marine biology, environmental radioactivity and applied wave research. One of the programmes destined for closure had been collecting quantitative data on sea water chemistry, temperature, fish and plankton abundance since the 1920s. Since this area of research is of the highest importance in assessing the eventual impact of global warming, it is hardly surprising that the Government's inadequate and inconsistent support drew heavy criticism.

The Agriculture and Food Research Council has suffered enormous cuts: it lost 25 per cent of its staff (2,052 permanent posts) between April 1983 and April 1989 (offset by about 600 temporary posts), with further losses of up to 660 posts forecast. These cuts have been due in part to the loss of research contracts commissioned by the Ministry of Agriculture, Fisheries and Food (MAFF), as the Government tried to reduce public funding of what is called 'near market' research. It is hard to discern whether industry has continued the projects; it is even harder to understand why such projects as certain research in listeria (which causes some type of food poisoning) and crypto-sporidium (a parasite increasingly affecting drinking water) were under threat as 'near market', and not deemed to be in the public interest.

Likewise, MAFF has plans to reduce its research staff by around 700 people (about one-third). 'Rationalisation' of its resources includes the closure of four experimental horti-culture stations and the much-criticised decision to move the National Fruit Collection, a genetic preserve of fruit species and varieties, from Kent to a new site at an existing college.

Underfunding and inconsistency can only create in-security among researchers.

Staff at the Freshwater Biological Association (FBA), whose headquarters is at Windermere, were faced with 'an enforced declaration in 1987 of a state of redundancy', as the FBA's 1989 Annual Report put it. Funding prospects seemed so insecure that the Report even contained an Appeal for donations to support the curation of the internationally important Fritsch collection, named after a founder of the FBA. This contains half a million illustrations and descriptions of freshwater algae, used as reference material for identification of species. One of the FBA's scientific study sites is currently faced with the prospect of sale, having already lost half its staff due to funding cuts in recent years. Its special equipment includes a fluvarium, unique in Britain, which is essentially a complete aquarium for freshwater studies through which flows a branch of the River Frome in Dorset.

# The Natural Environment Research Council

Alongside government departments – principally the Department of Education and Science (DES), the Department of the Environment and the Department of Energy – the Natural Environment Research Council (NERC) plays a key role in coordinating and conducting scientific work on environmental issues. It provides funding for several of its own institutes, such as the British Antarctic Survey, the British Geological Survey, the Institute of Hydrology and the Sea Mammal Research Unit, and also grant-aids other institutes and university research projects and students. The complex and unpredictable financial basis on which it has to operate illustrates and typifies the Government's failure to put environmental research on a sure footing.

NERC funding comes chiefly from the science budget administered by the DES, from research commissioned by other government departments or overseas governments, and from commercial contracts with the private sector.

NERC has made efforts to increase income from commissioned and commercial work, which provides roughly 25 per cent of income. Indeed, it now even has a corporate marketing strategy. Commissions from the UK Government are predicted to fall steadily through the next five year planning period. UK industrial support for NERC is negligible, and not expected to increase significantly. Private industry, for which the investigation of long-term environmental trends is hardly a pressing priority, can never provide a satisfactory resource base for fundamental research.

Accordingly, the bulk of NERC funding will continue to come from central government. Between the mid-1980s and 1988, science budget funding allocated by the DES declined by five per cent. 1989 saw a boost, because of special short term projects, but the long term trend is still downwards. NERC's 1990 Corporate Plan still assumes a 'declining overall' budget. In February 1989, NERC chairman John Knill admitted that an annual increase in funding of £12 million would be needed to reverse this long-term decline. As things stand, there is no guarantee of any improvement in the situation, which has already led to the loss of 600 environmental science posts since 1983 – a 20 per cent decrease (from 3,250 in 1983 to 2,650 in 1989). Increasing numbers of NERC staff hold temporary posts rather than permanent appointments, a trend NERC admits is likely to continue over the next five year planning period. This is a predictable response to the necessity of short-term planning imposed by unpredictable budgets and potentially changing priorities.

# Department of the Environment Research

In May and June 1988, the then Secretary of State for the Environment, Nicholas Ridley, gave figures, in replies to Parliamentary questions, outlining his Department's spending on environmental research and protection during the 1980s. The details covered five categories: radioactive

waste, air pollution, water, countryside and other environmental protection. The total spending declined between
1982 and 1985, and in 1987/8 was still less, in real terms,
than the 1981/2 level of £21.3 million. Almost half the
DoE's research budget has for some years been spent on
radioactive waste research. Since public concern about
environmental safety and protection was growing rapidly
all through these years, Mr Ridley's answer can only be
seen as an admission of his Department's failure: narrow
financial constraints clearly prevailed over the need to
maintain and improve the research programme.

There has been some improvement since then. Additional DoE resources were announced in December 1988, with
a total of £36 million for research in 1989/90. This sum
included support for water metering trials (50 per cent of
the costs: cynics might suggest that this was public funding
for the benefit of the soon-to-be-privatised water companies). Research into the North Sea marine environment
received a £0.6 million boost, and there was £0.45 million
extra for work on climate change. Other government
departments also help in these areas, contributing some £7
million towards North Sea research, for instance.

Of course, these funding boosts are welcome. It has to be
said, however, that the sums spent remain inadequate given
the gravity of the problems we now face.

The low priority given to vital research in the early and
mid-1980s is evident when we consider that the extra £0.45
million granted for climate change research in December
1988 represented a quadrupling of expenditure in that area
by the DoE. We must hope that Mrs Thatcher's publicly
stated commitment to climate research will lead to stable
and extended long-term funding becoming available.

The Government's White Paper on the Environment
drew much attention to the environmental research that is
funded (approximately £200 million currently). Whilst the
introductory summary stated an objective of 'increased

effort' on research and monitoring, there are no concrete proposals for increased funding. For instance, the Economic and Social Research Council's proposal for the establishment of a Global Environmental Research Centre receives mention, but as yet the allocation of any funds from central government has not been announced.

# Natural History Museum

Another institute stressed by financial worries is the Natural History Museum. Its work is at the very centre of international studies in evolution and taxonomy – the characterisation and classification of species, both contemporary and fossil. The Museum has the largest library of natural history books in the world, holds over 60 million plant, animal and mineral samples, and is used by researchers from all over the world.

The Museum's recent corporate plan has revealed plans to cut the scientific and curatorial staff by a further 15 per cent, or 50 out of 300 posts. Fifty jobs had already been lost since 1984. The Chairman of the Museum's Trustees, Sir Walter Bodmer, wrote in *Nature* (June 14th 1990): 'The essence of our financial problem is that the Government's "grant in aid" will not compensate adequately for inflation.' The Museum's Director has called for an extra £4.4 million over five years to eliminate the shortfall, but even this would only allow the museum to maintain its plans for a pruned programme.

'Museum's plans beyond belief' was the headline over the letters page of *Nature* (June 14th 1990), and a *Nature* editorial (May 3rd 1990) described these plans as 'a shabby document'. While shifts in climate are debated, while new possibilities of deriving important drugs from wild plants await investigation, while the process of evolution still holds surprises, the value of the Museum's research is incalculable. Yet it is planning to cut scientific staff and focus more resources on public exhibitions to make ends meet.

An interesting recent study of plant leaves shows how even dry herbarium specimens stored for years can yield important insights. One researcher looked at the number of pores on the leaves of plant specimens, many of which had been collected in the nineteenth century. These leaf pores take in the gas carbon dioxide, which, along with water and sunlight energy, then forms the food stores for plants. Many of the more recently collected specimens had fewer pores in the leaves, as had been predicted by correlation with estimated rising carbon dioxide levels in the atmosphere. The extent of global warming may still be debatable – but here we see a real anatomical response of plants to increased carbon dioxide levels. What else is going on as our atmosphere changes?

# Water industry research and 'clean coal'

In recent years, expert bodies have criticised the scale and direction of government-backed research in two key areas: water and 'clean coal'.

In 1986, a Long-Term Water Research Requirements Committee, reporting to the Department of the Environment, made no less than eighty proposals to rectify weaknesses in water research. A House of Lords Select Committee on Science and Technology had recommended development of a long-term strategy for water research because of concern that strategic research was 'at risk of being neglected'.

The Water Research Requirements Committee suggested that extra research might cost £3 million annually over five years in order to remedy the situation. They identified the areas in which the strategic research base was deficient. Many of these areas are of the plainest importance. They included the transfer and transformation of pollutants in the environment; basic research on toxicity in aquatic organisms; assessing the impact of sewage sludge disposal at sea; protecting water resources against pollution from waste disposal; and studying trace organic compounds in groundwater used for public supply.

Technologies to clean up emissions from coal-burning power stations ('clean coal' technologies) are of vital importance in the battle to reduce acid rain. Britain's research programme in this field is inadequate – especially when contrasted with that of Denmark, West Germany or Sweden. In 1986/7, the Department of Energy spent £0.4 million on 'clean coal' technology and the Central Electricity Generating Board spent £0.5 million on reduction of sulphur dioxide emissions. Small wonder, then, that the International Energy Agency (IEA), reporting on Britain's emission abatement programme in December 1987, was critical of the low priority accorded the work and of its poor coordination. The failure to set clear environmental standards, the IEA reported, deprived British research of a valuable stimulus.

When we recall the inadequacy of funding for renewable energy (the figure fell steadily in the years after 1981–82, though some welcome new projects have been announced recently), and when we contrast this with the vast sums still available for nuclear research (see the chapter on Energy), it is difficult not to feel that vested interests and institutional inertia, rather than a clear sense of environmental priorities, have dictated the pattern of research funding in energy.

The nuclear power programme gobbles up the lion's share of research and development funding from the Department of Energy. Its 1988/9 budget was five times that of non-nuclear research, and only half of the non-nuclear R&D money was spent on renewable energy

186

projects. The proportion of funds directed to non-nuclear R&D will increase as research on nuclear power declines in the early 90s, but Government plans show that nuclear R&D will still get four times as much money in 1992/3 as R&D on renewable energy sources.

In the context of static or declining public funding, the result has been an inadequate and poorly-focussed programme. Let us hope that things will now improve, as the public and the Government begin to realise how much is at stake.

*Friends of the Earth Policy Recommendations*
# Environmental Research

**1.** Funding to the Agriculture and Food Research Council and Natural Environment Research Council should be restored to allow replacement of the research posts lost during the 1980s.

**2.** Future financial support for environmental research should increase by a factor beyond the inflation rate.

**3.** The unique qualities of established long-term data-gathering projects should be recognised. Their funding should be guaranteed unless experts in the field agree to the ending of the project.

**4.** The Natural History Museum's decline should be halted immediately by increasing the funds available for basic research. The historic Victorian building in which it is housed should be maintained out of separate funds not related to the science budget.

# Chapter 12

# OVERSEAS AID AND THE TROPICAL RAINFORESTS

Rainforest destruction stands in the forefront of popular environmental concerns. The horrific statistics are well known. Nearly 50 per cent of all tropical rainforests have been destroyed, mostly since 1945. Commercial logging alone accounts each year for the destruction or serious degradation of 5 million hectares. At current rates of clearance, virtually all the accessible forests of West Africa, Southeast Asia and Central America will be gone by the end of the century.

For indigenous forest peoples and for the regional environment the impact is devastating, and it also disrupts the global climate.

This destruction of nature is utterly avoidable. The earthmoving machines and the huge saws, the roads driven into the heart of Amazonia, the jailing of representatives of tribal forest dwellers, the turning of timber into dollars 24 hours a day, are symptoms of economic inequality, greed for profit, and pressure from the banks and governments of the world's rich countries. All these factors encourage and enforce inappropriate and environmentally destructive development strategies. Figures for rainforest destruction need to be considered alongside figures for tropical country indebtedness.

Between 1982 and 1988, the debt-burdened countries of Latin America, Africa and Asia transferred a net \$144 billion to their commercial creditors alone.

Indebtedness forces governments to promote rapid, unsustainable exploitation of natural resources such as tropical forests. Forest lands satisfy First World demands for luxury goods, generate profits for transnational companies and enrich a small minority of the people in developing countries. Their exploitation contributes nothing to the real development needs of forest regions. The fate of tropical rainforests is a perfect instance of the social and environmental damage identified in the Brundtland Report's comment that, too often 'natural resources are used, not for development or to raise living standards, but to meet the financial requirements of industrialised country creditors.' (We return below to the Brundtland Report, published as *Our Common Future*, Oxford, 1987.)

Recent research in the Peruvian Amazon has revealed that non-timber products such as fruit, nuts and latex, represent over 90 per cent of the potential value of the forest's resources. The net present value of these products was put at around \$9,000 per hectare per year. The researchers calculated that if one hectare of forest was cut for timber on a once-only, non-sustainable basis, it would only yield the net sum of \$1,000. Even careful selective logging represented a danger to this economic potential, as damage to just 5 per cent of the fruit and latex trees would impair the forest's yields, reducing the net economic value of logging to zero.

# Aid, trade and debt

The struggle of indebted countries to pay off their creditors is bringing increasing environmental damage and human misery. Currently, developing countries are virtually forced into the short-term over-exploitation of their natural resources. Change can come only through a combination of debt reduction, increased overseas aid and coherent strategies for truly sustainable development.

Britain has a part to play, both in its own bilateral relations with developing countries and as a member of international organisations including the World Bank, the International Monetary Fund (IMF) and the European Community (EEC).

# Debt and its consequences

Poor countries trying to pay off loans have in recent years had to shoulder the double burden of rising interest rates and falling commodity prices. As loan repayments mount up and the terms of their trade with the industrialised world worsen, they are forced to borrow more money – and the spiral of debt continues. If they apply for new loans from the International Monetary Fund, they will probably have to comply with an 'adjustment programme'. This is likely to be to the detriment of environmental programmes, and will generally make life harder for the poor by insisting on cuts in social spending.

The effort to escape this spiral of rising debt pushes developing countries into unsustainable exploitation of their natural resources. Minerals and farmland, as well as tropical hardwoods, are regarded primarily as potential earners of foreign exchange. Cash crops for export – cotton, tea, coffee, tobacco – displace the subsistence crops once grown by small farmers, and the farmers themselves are pushed aside onto 'marginal' land (such as forest areas) as large-scale agribusiness moves in.

As the pattern repeats itself in country after country, commodity prices tend to fall because of over-supply. This may induce an even more frantic effort to 'mine the soil' – and to 'mine the forests'.

Ecological diversity suffers as forests, wetlands and savannahs shrink and disappear. The natural environment is further threatened by the lack of pollution control, sanitation and water treatment. Under austerity programmes, such provision is all too easily counted as a 'luxury'. But its absence threatens human health, as well as damaging the environment. Cholera, typhoid, dysentery and other avoidable diseases can all increase.

# The British aid programme

After the 1979 general election, Britain's Ministry of Overseas Development ceased to exist. Its responsibilities were taken on by the Overseas Development Administration (ODA), a subordinate part of the Foreign and Commonwealth Office.

Restrictions and cuts undermined the Overseas Development Administration's work throughout the early 1980s. Scientific units were particularly affected. Staff at the ODA's Land Resources Development Centre were pruned by 65 per cent, even though the House of Commons Foreign Affairs Committee produced a highly favourable report on the value of their work in 1983/4. Still harder hit was the ODA's Tropical Development and Research Unit which lost virtually all its personnel between 1980 and 1985.

The Government has also cut the sum spent directly on overseas aid. In 1982/3 there was a cut of £20 million (11 per cent). Since then the budget has risen slowly in nominal terms – so slowly that it has barely remained static in real terms and has fallen as a proportion of GNP. In the financial year 1988, for example, the increase of £360 million on the previous year's figure of £1.7 billion failed to keep pace with inflation.

The overall consequences are that aid spending in real

191

terms is not much more than three-quarters of the 1979 level, a fact which shames the Government and the country.

By international standards, our record is poor. The British aid budget is smaller as a percentage of GNP than that of most other countries in the OECD (Organisation for Economic Co-operation and Development – a grouping of 25 developed countries, including the UK, USA, Canada and Japan). At 0.32 per cent of GNP, it is less than half the level of 0.7 per cent advocated as a minimum target by the United Nations.

Recently, there have been some signs of greater Government interest in aid and development. Chris Patten, as Minister at the Overseas Development Administration, earned some credit from environmentalists when, in 1988, he met with the Chief of the Brazilian Kaiapo Indians to discuss the threatened flooding of their homeland by a dam funded by the World Bank. There has been more consultation between civil servants and the non-governmental organisations (NGOs) which play an important fundraising, campaigning and educational role. The establishment of a Natural Resources and Environment Department at the ODA in 1986 was a welcome step: the Chief Natural Resources Adviser is supported by specialist advisers on agriculture, animal health, fisheries, forestry and the environment.

The signing of a Memorandum of Understanding on cooperation on environmental issues between the UK Government and the Government of Brazil, one of Chris Pattern's last acts as Minister of Overseas Development, was a positive indication of the Government's willingness to work with tropical countries not usually covered by the aid programme. The Memorandum essentially offered financial and technical support for research into forest management aimed at sustaining long-term productivity and regrowth of timber resources.

In November 1989, the Prime Minister announced a

further £100 million in bilateral aid to 'tropical forestry activities, over the next three years, mostly within the framework of the Tropical Forestry Action Plan' (TFAP). This increase in expenditure on tropical forest-related programmes was welcome, but it ignored criticisms from Friends of the Earth and other environmental groups who had long argued that the TFAP was fundamentally flawed in its approach to *conserving* rainforests. In June 1990, a high-level official review vindicated these concerns and found that the TFAP had encouraged the expansion of destructive commercial logging 'in a number of countries'; that the performance of the UN Food and Agriculture Organisation, responsible for coordinating the TFAP, had 'fallen far short of reasonable expectations'; that there had been 'serious shortcomings' and 'no quality control' in many of the TFAP exercises; and that there had been 'inadequate consultation with those interested in and affected by forest policy', such as environmental groups, indigenous forest people, and other local communities.

To its credit, the Government has responded to these criticisms. In the White Paper on the Environment, *This Common Inheritance*, the Government called for reforms to the TFAP which would increase the Plan's emphasis on conservation, allow for greater involvement of local people, and address the policies which encourage forest destruction.

To date, the UK Government has not sought measures to counter the possibily destructive impact of national forestry plans already drawn up under the TFAP, nor to consider a moratorium on further funding for TFAP until the necessary reforms of the Plan are enacted.

# Multilateral aid and trade

International Monetary Fund adjustment schemes and

World Bank lending programmes often needlessly damage Third World ecosystems and override the rights of local people.

Even though the UK Government has reduced interest rates on official loans to some of the poorest African countries, and in some cases has written off debt, Britain continues to support IMF programmes without pressing for the inclusion of social and environmental objectives and safeguards. Nor has Britain acknowledged the need for complementary 'adjustment' here in the First World, where rich countries' policies on agriculture, energy and industry have all exacerbated global and Third World difficulties.

Mrs Thatcher is on record as supporting the inclusion of environmental sustainability as one objective of aid projects, yet when Nigel Lawson (then Chancellor of the Exchequer) spoke at a meeting of the World Bank in September 1989 he did not even mention the environment.

Through its Executive Directors on the World Bank's board, the UK is in a position directly to influence policy. The Directors should be given clear mandates, and they should be given adequate time – to fully consider the environmental and social implications of the many projects they are asked to decide upon. They should also be explicitly instructed to oppose any programme likely to have adverse environmental consequences, and to press for full involvement of local and tribal peoples in project decisions. Planning documents for aid projects should be available to the public, and both Parliament and the general public should be able to examine the British voting record on multilateral lending schemes.

The EC's Common Agricultural Policy (CAP) has flooded the world market with heavily subsidised surpluses of European sugar and other commodities, depressing prices and thereby reducing Third World foreign exchange earnings. While the UK has insisted that subsidies and protectionism should end, it has not hitherto stressed the need to highlight environmental considerations in deciding on the future of CAP. Both CAP and the General Agreement on Tarifs and Trade (GATT) can and should become forums in which to hammer out a new pattern of sustainable and equitable agriculture and agricultural trade. Again, British representatives on these bodies need a clear mandate if the Government's declared commitment to environmentally sound development is to be made effective.

# Sustainable development

The term invites political debate, but few would dispute the need for 'sustainable development' in the broadest sense – development that brings the people of poor countries lasting improvements in their quality of life, and which does not depend on short-term over-exploitation of such natural resources as farmland, forests and minerals. The Brundtland Commission (an international body under the auspices of the UN, chaired by Norwegian Prime Minister, Gro Harlem Brundtland) insisted on the need for aid programmes to promote sustainability. Its Report advocated special funding to restore and improve ecological bases for development and to strengthen developing countries' professional and institutional expertise in relevant disciplines.

The UK's response to Brundtland was widely regarded as inept. 'Smugness, not engagement, is its dominant tone,' commented the *Daily Telegraph* (August 3rd 1988). 'Britain has responded to Brundtland's letter, not its spirit.' However, Chris Patten, as Minister at the Overseas Development Administration, did state publicly that environmental factors should 'enter as by right into the complex of calculations which lie behind aid in whatever form'.

195

In March 1989, the Overseas Development Administration produced a new manual for the appraisal and implementation of aid projects, aiming to ensure that the British aid programme supported sustainable development. This document was widely circulated to non-governmental organisations and other interested groups, and their comments were taken note of in the preparation of the final text. But the revised version still has a major flaw: it is concerned with mitigating the environmental effects of aid projects, but makes no provision for outright rejection of a project on the grounds of excessive environmental damage.

# Tropical Rainforests

Of the 20 million hectares of tropical rainforest destroyed each year, logging accounts for about a quarter. Other destructive pressures come from cattle ranching, conversion to agriculture, and inappropriate development projects such as dams, roads and settlement schemes. The proposed (but successfully opposed) Xingu hydroelectric scheme that threatened the Kaiapo Indians in Brazil would have flooded an area of rainforest the size of Wales and displaced thousands of people. Such dam projects can also bring increases in water-borne diseases, disruption of rainfall cycles and changes in the climate (locally and, potentially, on an international scale), water pollution and soil erosion. The proposed Xingu scheme was defeated, but the Brazilian power industry has prepared plans for a total of 70 new hydroelectric dams in the Amazon region – displacing an estimated 500,000 people.

One Brazilian dam that did go ahead, the Balbina project, was admitted by the World Bank to have been 'ill-conceived'. This huge lake measuring 1,900 square kilometres is on average about 20 feet deep, and will generate only about 200 megawatts of electricity. This makes it hugely inefficient, even by the standards of some other Brazilian dam projects. The rotting vegetation in the shallow basin is expected to cause severe water quality problems, both ecologically and in engineering terms for the turbines. In consequence even less power may be generated than had been planned.

At present, logging is almost always carried out indiscriminately and with little attempt to contain its destructiveness. Present logging practice leaves surviving trees irreparably damaged and paves the way for wholesale forest destruction. Sustained-yield management – the planned cropping and replanting of forests to give yields that can be maintained indefinitely – is almost unknown in the tropics, and reforestation of any kind is rare. According to the International Tropical Timber Organisation (ITTO, a trade organisation whose aims include 'sustainable management of tropical timber resources' and 'market transparency and trade diversification'), less than one-eighth of one percent of tropical moist forests are being managed for the sustainable production of timber.

Britain must accept some of the responsibility. After Japan, Europe is the major market for internationally traded tropical hardwood, and Britain is one of Europe's largest importers. In 1988, woods imported into Britain included iroko from the Ivory Coast, mahogany from Brazil, ramin from Indonesia, meranti from Malaysia and lauan from the Philippines. Uses of hardwood include furniture, doors, window frames, construction, boat building and coffins.

# Toll of destruction: Brazil and Sarawak

The opening up of the rainforest has brought a massive

influx of gold prospectors into the north-western Amazon region. Up to 1,500 Yanomani Indians have died of infectious diseases brought in by outsiders. In May 1990, the Brazilian Government resorted to the blowing up of illegal airstrips, of which there are thought to have been more than 70, in a desperate attempt to protect the forest and its inhabitants.

Logging in Sarawak, Borneo, has recently been the subject of special investigations by an international mission headed by Lord Cranbrook of Britain's Nature Conservancy Counil. The mission, which visited Borneo at the request of the Malaysian Government, reported in May 1990 to a meeting of the International Tropical Timber Organisation. In Sarawak, too, tribal people are suffering as their traditional lifestyle is disrupted.

We used to be able to find wild boar and other animals in just a few minutes,' one Penan tribesman told a *Times* reporter (May 10th 1990). 'Now we can hunt for days and find nothing. We have to walk much further for the fruit trees and plants we have always used. The logging is destroying them. That's why we are trying to stop the logging.

Scarcity of wild plants and animals all too easily leads to their outright extinction. We are now seeing species destruction at a rate 'never before witnessed on the planet', says the Brundtland report. As many as 50 species a day may be being wiped out. Often, there will have been no opportunity for scientists to classify them or assess their potential value to humankind. Rare wildlife at risk in Sarawak includes the orangutan, eight different kinds of hornbill birds, gliding snakes and flying foxes. The Government of Sarawak (a partially autonomous State of Malaysia) has committed itself to declaring 8 per cent of the country a protected area, but as yet only one quarter of the promised area has been so designated.

Worldwide, there may be more than 10,000 different species of tropical forest trees. Only a few have any commercial value as timber. Yet indiscriminate logging puts all this incredible diversity at risk.

# Safeguards and reforms

Britain supports both the International Tropical Timber Organisation and the Tropical Forestry Action Plan (TFAP). The TFAP is jointly promoted by the World Bank and the UN Food and Agriculture Organisation. These initiatives claim to be advancing the conservation, sustainable management and restoration of tropical rainforests. However, effective action has been slow. As we saw above, the TFAP has been widely criticised. More radical programmes need to be adopted, urgently.

In November 1990, the UK put forward a proposal to the ITTO for a feasibility study into the labelling of tropical timber. This had been prepared by Friends of the Earth and the Oxford Forestry Institute. Ministers at the Foreign Office, the Department of the Environment, the Department of Trade and Industry and the Overseas Development Administration have all recognised the value of labelling 'approved timbers', so that consumers can choose wood that comes from sustainably managed sources and has been extracted with due environmental care.

When some timber producing countries made clear their opposition to labelling, the UK representative was persuaded to amend the proposal. Although specific references to labelling were removed, the Government has given reassurances that it will be considered in the study, which will investigate the more general timber trade links between rainforest and consumer.

A recent indication of the Government's concern with rainforest conservation was the £1 million matching grant which the ODA gave the World Wide Fund for Nature in February 1989 to support its tropical forest conservation work.

Trade reform within the EEC also has an important part to play in encouraging imports from sustainably managed forests and prohibiting those from regions where wholesale forest destruction is the norm. Through its importation of tropical hardwoods, its aid programme and its members' special relationships with many African, Caribbean and Pacific countries, the EEC has a key role to play. Europe's trade and aid policies can both contribute to the protection of rainforests and encourage sustainable development.

The need for such measures was recognised in the EEC's Fourth Environmental Action Programme, which called for 'a re-examination of the trade and aid policies of both the Community and Member States from the standpoint of their impact on tropical forest conservation and the promotion of a code of conduct among timber companies based in the Community.' Such measures have been supported on a number of occasions by the European Parliament and, following its investigation into the EEC role in tropical forest issues, more recently by the House of Lords in Britain.

However, in May 1990, the Minister for Overseas Development, Lynda Chalker, gave her approval to an EEC Council of Development Ministers resolution on tropical forests which signally failed either to address the EEC's unique role in influencing tropical forest exploit-ation, or to promote any new EEC initiatives. Despite growing concerns over TFAP, which had been explicitly recognised by Lynda Chalker only twelve days prior to the meeting, the Ministers resolved to increase EEC support for the Plan. Instead of considering measures to regulate the EEC's imports of tropical hardwoods, the EEC was to give extra support to International Tropical Timber Organisation, the principle objective of which is to 'expand

and diversify' the international trade in tropical timbers. No proposals were put forward to control the activities of European-based companies in other industrial sectors, such as mining and construction, which have detrimental impacts upon tropical forests.

Recent European and British initiatives have nonetheless begun to address the rainforest crisis. Britain's role in multilateral and international institutions will offer further opportunities for action – if the will is there.

*Friends of the Earth Policy Recommendations*

# Overseas Aid and the Tropical Rainforests

The following policies must be adopted by the Government in order to take further the limited reforms so far carried out through the Overseas Development Administration to promote sustainable development, and in particular the conservation of tropical rainforests.

**1.** The Government should increase the aid budget to at least the UN target of 0.7 per cent of GNP. *(Reiterated as 'Global Warming' Policy Recommendation #11)*

**2.** A high proportion of the aid budget should be spent on the sustainable management of renewable natural resources, and on protecting endangered ecosystems such as wetlands and rainforests. *(Reiterated as 'Global Warming' Policy Recommendation #12)*

201

**3.** The Government should ensure that Britain supports only those multilateral development projects, including those funded by the World Bank and International Monetary Fund, which are environmentally sustainable and do not destroy the homelands or infringe the rights of tribal peoples.

**4.** The Government should strengthen debt initiatives aimed at helping the poorest countries in sub-Saharan Africa and elsewhere. Britain should press for more substantial relief on debts owed to such agencies as the World Bank and European Development Fund – including outright cancellation of bad debts. Such initiatives should be directed towards middle-income Third World nations, as well as the poorest.

**5.** The Government should support European legislation to ensure that all hardwood imports come from sustainably managed forests. This should include support for the establishment of an EEC fund to assist sustainable forest management plans. (*Reiterated as 'Global Warming' Policy Recommendation #13*)

**6.** The Government should promote the listing of endangered and threatened tree species under the Convention on International Trade in Endangered Species (CITES), to which Britain is a signatory. This imposes a duty to control the trade and importation of listed species.

**7.** European and international trade agreements (such as the General Agreement on Tariffs and Trade, GATT) should enshrine policies for environmental sustainability.

**8.** A moratorium on funding of the Tropical Forestry Action Plan should be implemented pending reforms to promote an accountable, multi-sectoral programme for tropical rainforest conservation.

# Chapter 13

# OUT OF THE GREENHOUSE: BRITAIN AND GLOBAL WARMING

Five years ago, hardly anybody knew or cared about global warming. Today, leading politicians, the popular press, serious journalists and most of the scientific community are united in stressing the urgency of the crisis.

Scientists have long known that the delicate balance of gases in the atmosphere traps heat from the sun that would otherwise be lost to space. The atmosphere acts rather like the glass in a greenhouse. This natural 'greenhouse effect' keeps the Earth at a habitable temperature.

This balance is now being upset by the impact of human activity. As we burn coal, oil and gas, destroy forests on a massive scale, and adopt new patterns of agriculture, we are steadily increasing the concentrations of greenhouse gases in the atmosphere. These include carbon dioxide, methane and nitrous oxide. The chlorofluorocarbons (CFCs) which are damaging the ozone layer are also very powerful greenhouse gases. If concentrations continue to rise, more heat will be trapped and average temperatures will increase worldwide. The world's climate may be dramatically affected, for this additional heat could affect not just temperatures, but rainfall and storm patterns too. Global warming will cause the oceans to expand and land-based glaciers to melt, and this will raise sea levels.

Climate disruption and rising sea levels might combine to bring catastrophe to some of the world's poorest and most vulnerable countries. Bangladesh, China, Egypt and low-lying islands in the Indian and Pacific Oceans are all at risk. The Maldives, for example, are only six feet above sea level. Millions of people face threats to their homes, their livelihoods, and their lives.

People in Britain have been concerned by the extra-ordinary weather conditions we have encountered during 1989 and 1990: exceptionally mild winters, savage gales, record temperatures, and serious summer drought in the southern part of the country. When ferocious February winds followed hard upon some of the warmest February weather ever recorded, the *Daily Telegraph* (February 28th 1990) noted: 'For the first time people are seriously questioning whether or not we are on the rough edges of the much-forecast Greenhouse Effect.'

Recent exceptional weather may not have been a consequence of global warming, but the ferocity of the February 1990 storms was a foretaste of what dramatic climate change might entail. And we have been reminded that long, hot, dry summers might mean recurrent water shortages and other threats to crops and health in Britain.

It has become clear, in short, that we must take action or risk the gravest consequences.

# The scientists' view

Atmospheric concentrations of carbon dioxide ($CO_2$, the major greenhouse gas) are estimated to have increased by 25 per cent in the last century, a change on a scale not seen since the end of the last Ice Age. Scientists have debated the extent of the effects that the build up of this and other gases are likely to have on world climate.

An international scientific consensus has now emerged from the work of the United Nations Intergovernmental Panel on Climate Change (IPCC). The IPCC's Science Report has settled recent scientific debate on the seriousness and urgency of the issues. The report, prepared by 300 scientists, stressed that the longer we wait before taking action, the worse the problems will get. Commenting on the IPCC Science Report, Mrs Thatcher said: 'Governments and international organisations in every part of the world are going to have to sit up and take notice and respond.'

The IPCC report predicted temperature rises of about one degree centigrade higher than now by 2025 and three degree centigrade before the end of the next century, if trends in greenhouse gas emissions continue as they are now. A two degree rise would make the world hotter than at any time for 125,000 years. Scientists are particularly concerned by a predicted rate of warming which is greater than that seen over the last 10,000 years.

Global sea level rise for 'business as usual' greenhouse gas emissions will be about 20 centimetres by 2030 and 65 centimetres by the end of the next century, rising at a rate three to six times faster than that seen over the last 100 years.

The second IPCC report on the impacts of global warming warns of a number of possible severe effects. Agriculture in some regions may suffer from changes in weather, diseases, pests and weeds. Areas where farming is only just possible today are at greatest risk. Trees and other species may not be able to cope with rapid climate change. Water supplies would be under threat: large parts of Africa, Southeast Asia, India, Central America, Brazil and the Mediterranean area of Europe are among those areas at greatest risk. Drought, storms and flooding are dire threats. Heat stress and the spread of diseases such as

malaria could threaten public health. But in the words of
the IPCC report: 'The gravest effects of climate change may
be those on human migration as millions are displaced by
shoreline erosion, coastal flooding and severe drought.'
Millions of refugees could then find themselves without
proper health facilities – a recipe for epidemics sweeping
through refugee camps and into local communities.

The IPCC's work has been a turning point. Britain and a
number of other countries had been arguing that it was
premature to decide on policy until the scientists' verdict
was in. Now, delay can no longer be excused.

# What has to be done?

The best way to counter the threat of global warming is to
cut emissions of greenhouse gases. The IPCC study
concluded that to keep the atmosphere the way it is now
would require cuts in current carbon dioxide emissions of
over 60 per cent. Deep cuts would also have to be made in
emissions of CFCs and nitrous oxide, the other long-lived
greenhouse gases.

Energy production and use is without doubt one of the
vitally important areas for radical policy changes. A full
review of the issues, with recommendations for action, can
be found in the chapter on Energy. Here, we will summarise some of the key points.

The development of renewable energy sources (such as
wind, wave and solar power), which produce negligible
greenhouse emissions, must be promoted. In Britain,
unfortunately, the Government gives little backing to the
necessary research. The White Paper on the Environment
claimed that the Government has 'supported the development of a wide range of renewable technologies over the last
decade' but, in fact, the Government's funding for renewable energy research and development in the last 10 years

has averaged less than £20 million per year. In contrast, funding for nuclear research and development has averaged in excess of £200 million per year.

A higher target for electricity generation from renewable energy sources was announced in the White Paper. Generating capacity should reach 1,000 megawatts, up from a target of 600 megawatts, in the year 2000. This was a welcome step, but this target falls way short of the total potential capacity. Renewable energy projects submitted to the Department of Energy by the beginning of 1990 had identified a total of 2,000 megawatts potential capacity.

Even more crucial than the development of renewables is the pursuit of energy efficiency. More efficient use of energy will lead to dramatic cuts in greenhouse gas emissions. There is scope for major improvements using readily available technology.

However, the Government continues to give energy efficiency a low priority. In November 1989, the Department of Energy, commenting on a report on global warming prepared by the all-party House of Commons Energy Committee, stated: 'The Government believes that, since energy efficiency is above all a matter for decisions and actions by individuals. . . then the best way forward is through the operation of the market, lubricated by information and advice.' In other words, the Government was itself unwilling to do very much to promote energy efficiency.

While claiming it wants to give 'a renewed boost' to energy efficiency in the White Paper, the Government prefers to rely on the operation of the market and decisions made by individuals. The White Paper included a 'wish-list' of activities to promote energy efficiency, but this was not accompanied by any increase in resources for the Energy Efficiency Office. The increase in budget for the Energy Efficiency Office for 1991 is due to the Home Energy Efficiency Scheme, which is a replacement of (rather than a development of) existing grants to low-income households for energy efficiency measures. The Office's budget has fallen by half in real terms since its peak in 1986.

Despite much discussion of energy efficiency, the Government has taken only two modest steps beyond the general promotion of energy efficiency in its White Paper. The Government now accepts a long-standing European Community proposal for a labelling scheme for electrical appliances providing information on their efficiency, and the introduction of minimum efficiency standards for a range of electrical appliances. But even here the Government prefers voluntary schemes to legislation, even though an Energy Efficiency Office report for the Government doubted the value of this approach.

Electricity privatisation has been the keystone of recent government energy policy. The regulatory framework for the new electricity companies gives them no compelling incentive to invest in the efficient use of energy. On the contrary: the more electricity they sell, the more money they will make – and the more polluting greenhouse gases they will produce.

The fastest growing source of carbon dioxide emissions in Britain today is petrol and diesel burnt in cars and lorries. This highlights the fact that transport is a crucial aspect of energy policy. Again, a detailed analysis of the problems and of the Government's inadequate response is given in the chapter on Transport: here, we simply summarise the key points.

Mrs Thatcher said in March 1990: 'We are not going to do without a great car economy.' Her enthusiasm for the motor vehicle, and her reluctance to develop alternative public transport, have been shared by successive Secretaries of State for Transport. Challenged on the global warming threat from cars, Cecil Parkinson stated that no substantial cuts in emissions could be achieved before the year 2010. Notoriously, the Department of Transport stands by its May 1989 projections that road traffic will increase by betwen 83 and 142 per cent by 2025 – which could put no less than 20 million additional cars on our roads. The average car not only produces around four times its own weight in carbon dioxide every year, it also generates other gases which contribute to global warming and air pollution. And it is worth recalling that catalytic converters do not remove carbon dioxide from vehicle exhausts.

All in all, the 'great car economy' is also a 'great greenhouse gas economy'. Yet the Government is not only committed to the car, it even seems unable to take measures to 'civilise the motor car', as the Secretry of State for Transport, Mr Parkinson, has claimed he wishes to do. No fuel efficiency standards have been set for vehicles. The company car tax perk, worth an estimated £2 billion a year, has not been abolished. The only specific measure for which the Government can claim credit is a requirement that car engines must be tuned and tested for emissions at the annual MOT test and improved enforcement of existing national speed limits.

The record is no better in other related policy areas. On CFCs, the Government has gone along (tardily enough) with agreed international programmes, but has not acted to ban CFC production in Britain. Our miserly record on overseas aid – Britain spends less than half the UN's recommended figure of 0.7 per cent of GNP on aid – prevents us from offering developing countries the substantial help they need to pursue efficient, environmentally benign solutions to their energy problems.

Research and international meetings have been a soft option for the Government. Britain put £750,000 into the work of the IPCC, and its science working group was chaired by John Houghton, the Director of the UK Meteorological Office. Some £6 million was allocated for climate prediction in 1989–90, and in May 1990 the Hadley Centre for Climate Prediction and Research was opened. Mrs Thatcher held a global warming seminar in Downing Street in April 1989 to give key members of the Government a crash course in the subject. Judging by Ministers' responses in making policy, the seminar had little influence.

Britain's approach to forest conservation, another vital tool in the struggle to control global warming, has been to support the Tropical Forestry Action Plan (TFAP). Most of the £100 million we are to spend on tropical forest conservation, as promised by Mrs Thatcher in her speech to the UN in November 1989, will go to TFAP. Friends of the Earth has been very critical of the Action Plan, which has not succeeded in stopping deforestation: in fact, the rate of forest destruction has speeded up since TFAP was implemented in 1985. Britain's financial contribution will be of use only if TFAP is reformed. This point was conceded in the Environment White Paper, where the Government recognises that the TFAP needs reform. The potential benefits of a successful conservation strategy are considerable: growing trees take carbon dioxide out of the atmosphere, and forests act as a valuable carbon store. Humanity's current destruction of forests not only squanders an invaluable natural resource, it accounts for approximately one fifth of current global emissions of carbon dioxide.

# Has Britain 'taken the lead internationally'?

Global warming is indeed a global threat. Atmosphere and climate do not respect national boundaries. But this does not mean that we should wait for worldwide agreement before taking appropriate action. Waiting for such agreement would simply be a recipe for delay.

The industrialised countries, including Britain, must act first, as they bear the heaviest responsibility for greenhouse gas emissions. In a major report on global warming published in July 1989, the House of Commons Energy Committee rightly argued that 'the UK should set an example to the world by seriously tackling its own emission problems in advance of international understanding: the world response will be the sum of individual countries' respones.' Three months later, Mrs Thatcher claimed that we were indeed setting such an example: in combatting global warming, she told the Conservative Party Conference, 'Britain has taken the lead internationally and we shall continue to do so'.

If 'taking the lead' means implementing appropriate policies in energy use, transport and other related fields, we have already seen that the Prime Minister's claim is a hollow one.

Nor has Britain's record been particularly admirable at international conferences. In June 1988, Britain attended the Toronto Conference which identified a global target of 20 per cent reductions in carbon dioxide emissions by the year 2005. In November 1989, however, Britain was one of a handful of countries which blocked international consensus on a much more modest target: to hold carbon dioxide emissions where they are now by 2000. Ten European nations were ready to commit themselves to this more modest goal at Washington in February 1990, but Britain refused to join them. At the Bergen conference on Environment and Development in May 1990, Britain was again in a minority by refusing to agree to stabilisation of carbon dioxide emissions at present levels by the year 2000.

Mrs Thatcher's public rhetoric has hardly been consistent with this British reluctance to support effective international action. She has repeatedly drawn world attention to the gravity of the problem. Her major speech to the United Nations in November 1989 was couched in dramatic language:

> What we are doing now to the world, by degrading the land surfaces, by polluting the waters and by adding greenhouse gases to the air at an unprecedented rate – all this is new in the experience of the Earth . . . Whole areas of our planet could be subject to drought and starvation . . . as a result of the destruction of forests and the accumulation of greenhouse gases.

She has returned to them since. At the opening the Hadley Centre for Climate Prediction and Research in May 1990, she insisted that global warming 'is not something arcane or remote from every day concerns . . . The problems don't lie in the future, they are here and now: and it is our children and grandchildren, who are already growing up, who will be affected.' Just before the IPCC report was published, in the same month, she spoke once more of 'fundamental changes which will alter our way of life'. 'We simply must follow the advice of the scientists', she continued, 'if we are to preserve the most precious heritage we have.'

But when Britain finally set its own target for control of carbon dioxide emissions in May 1990, after months of pressure at home and from European partners, it was obvious that all the rhetoric had given birth to unambitious and inadequate policy. On the very same day that the IPCC scientists indicated that carbon dioxide emission cuts of at least 60 per cent would be needed to stabilise atmospheric concentrations, Mrs Thatcher announced that we would stabilise emissions at 1990 levels by the year 2005 – and then only if other countries were also prepared to commit themselves.

This target was far weaker than that proposed at Toronto

in 1988, and weaker than any put forward at subsequent international conferences. The Prime Minister would not say which other nations had to agree.

Friends of the Earth's verdict on the target as totally inadequate was quickly echoed by newspaper editorials. 'An inadequate response' was the verdict of the *Independent* (May 26th 1990); 'Britain's declared position', commented *The Times*, 'means increased concentrations of $CO_2$ for another generation. If Mrs Thatcher really accepts the existing scientific evidence, should she not bring her policy into line?' (May 26th 1990). And the *Financial Times* (May 29th 1990) also took the view that 'Mrs Thatcher's actions are out of tune with her words'.

As well as failing the environment, the Government's stated target for carbon dioxide emissions does a disservice to British industry. At a time when our European partners are aiming for more challenging goals, similar objectives should be set here. The Government has failed to guide investment by making the necessary policy decisions in energy and transport policy.

The Government has not been able to provide any detailed justification for adopting this inadequate target. On June 3rd 1990, in response to the widespread criticism that had greeted the announcement, Mrs Thatcher said merely that stabilisation of carbon dioxide emissions at 1990 levels by 2005 was 'what we can do'. John Wakeham told Parliament that 'the Prime Minister has taken the lead' with what he persisted in calling 'a demanding target'. To make matters worse, the Government has emphasised the 'pain and anguish' involved in controlling greenhouse emissions, and has said nothing about the savings that would accrue from lower energy consumption or the other benefits to the environment (for example helping to tackle smog and acid rain) which would flow from a programme to combat global warming.

The real 'pain and anguish' will come if targets as modest

as Britain's are allowed to become the norm. Study of the IPCC reports makes it quite clear that stabilisation at current levels will not be enough to control global warming.

If Britain is leading the world, it is leading it in the wrong direction.

# Our European partners

The majority of European Community states want a common target of stabilising carbon dioxide emission levels by 2000, five years ahead of the British date. Carlo Ripa di Meana, the EEC Environment Commissioner, has called on Britain to bring its goal into line with this wider programme.

Britain (along with Spain, Portugal and Greece) has obstructed efforts to reach consensus on a European Community position. The Government has stood out no less than five times against the adoption of a common EEC target for carbon dioxide emissions: at the Noordwijk conference, at an IPCC meeting in February 1990, at the May 1990 Bergen conference, and twice (March and June 1990) at European Council of Environment Minister meetings.

West Germany, the Netherlands and Denmark have been setting the pace when it comes to national responses to global warming. Other countries with policies more advanced than Britain's include Sweden and Norway. The facts betray Britain's claim to be taking the lead.

The Netherlands will hold emissions steady a full ten years ahead of Britain, and will commence reducing carbon dioxide emissions by 2000. Its outline plan to meet this objective includes energy efficiency measures, switching to less polluting fuels, backing public transport and promoting waste recycling.

Measures announced by Denmark include bans on new

coal-fired power stations and new energy efficiency standards for buildings and electrical appliances. The Danes aim for 20 per cent cuts in carbon dioxide emissions by 2005.

West Germany has a more productive economy and a larger population than Britain. Yet it has agreed to reduce, not stabilise, carbon dioxide emissions by 25 per cent from 1987 levels by the year 2005, going much further than Britain. This target does not include a target for the grossly inefficient economy of East Germany (newly unified with West Germany), where there is great scope for savings.

We should be aiming to equal or exceed these goals, instead of standing in the way of the necessary action. In its study *Getting out of the Greenhouse: An Agenda for UK Energy Policy* (1989), Friends of the Earth has shown that as a first step towards the major reductions in carbon dioxide emissions that we need, Britain could embark now on a programme to achieve at least 20 per cent cuts. Similar action will be needed on methane and nitrous oxide, and an early CFC ban should also be introduced.

None of this will happen if the Government clings to its belief that the marketplace and energy privatisation will solve our problems. They will not. Giving rein to the 'great car economy', preparing to sell British Coal and British Rail, and continuing to eschew intervention and regulation amounts to an agenda for inaction. If Britain is to play its part in combatting global warming, forceful government initiatives, including regulation and legislation, are needed now. A priority is to establish a target based on what is best for the environment, not one based on protecting privatisation programmes.

*Friends of the Earth Policy Recommendations*
# Global Warming

1.   The Government should introduce measures to encourage energy conservation and efficiency, to result in an annual reduction of national energy consumption of at least 1 per cent per year, starting now. This will require major improvements in building standards, legally binding minimum efficiency standards for mandatory appliances and a comprehensive scheme for the labelling of all energy-consuming goods.

Through grants and tax incentives (for instance linking mortgage tax relief to the energy efficiency of the home), the Government should promote the widest possible use of state-of-the-art energy-efficient technologies. It should take particular care to use them in its own buildings. *[Reiterated as 'Energy' Policy Recommendation #1, partly as 'Eco-labelling' Policy Recommendation #2]*

2.   The Energy Efficiency Office should be expanded to coordinate a national energy efficiency programme, including Combined Heat and Power schemes and district heating schemes. *[Reiterated as 'Energy' Policy Recommendation #2]*

3.   The Government should restructure the electricity and gas industries into energy service industries in which energy efficiency investments are profitable. *[Reiterated as 'Energy' Policy Recommendation #3]*

4.   The Government should reinstate and widen the scope of energy efficiency grants, targetting full grant support at low income households.

5.   The tax subsidy for company cars should be

abolished at the next budget. *[Reiterated as 'Air Pollution' Policy Recommendation #4, 'Transport', Policy Recommendation #3]*

**6.** Car use should be controlled by building up public transport, to prevent gains from pollution control being wiped out by the increase in the number of cars. *[Reiterated as 'Air Pollution' Policy Recommendation #5]*

**7.** Vehicle Excise Duty should be scrapped and incorporated into petrol tax. *[Reiterated as 'Transport' Policy Recommendation #4]*

**8.** Fuel efficiency standards should be adopted, with a goal of increasing current efficiency by 50 per cent by 2000 and 100 per cent by 2010.

**9.** The Government should implement a national programme to phase out the production and consumption of ozone-damaging CFCs, halons and methyl chloroform (with the vast majority going by 1992, bar essential medical uses and some existing refrigeration use); and confine HCFC use to essential applications and set an early phase-out date. *[Reiterated as 'Air Pollution' Policy Recommendation #6]*

**10.** Compulsory labelling and recycling schemes for products that still contain CFCs should be introduced. The Government should also levy a 'polluter pays' tax from CFC producers to raise funds for technology transfer to help developing countries to meet their needs without using CFCs. *[Reiterated as 'Air Pollution' Policy Recommendation #7]*

**11.** The Government should increase the aid budget to at least the UN target of 0.7 per cent of GNP. *[Reiterated as 'Overseas Aid and the Tropical Rainforests' Policy Recommendation #1]*

**12.** A high proportion of the aid budget should be spent on the sustainable management of renewable natural resources, and on protecting endangered ecosystems such as wetlands and rainforests. *[Reiterated as 'Overseas Aid and the Tropical Rainforests' Policy Recommendation #2]*

**13.** The Government should support European legislation to ensure that all hardwood imports come from sustainably managed forests. This should include support for the establishment of an EEC fund to assist sustainable forest management plans. *[Reiterated as 'Overseas Aid and the Tropical Rainforests' Policy Recommendation #5]*

# FURTHER READING

The ENDS Report
Monthly digest on environmental policy.
Environmental Data Services Ltd.
Telephone: 071 278 7624

## FRIENDS OF THE EARTH PUBLICATIONS:

The following publications can be ordered from:
    Friends of the Earth
    Publications Despatch Department
    26–28 Underwood Street
    London N1 7JQ

Price includes postage and packing. Please include payment with order and quote code number.

GOVERNMENT POLICY

*Stealing Our Future*
Friends of the Earth's critique of *This Common Inheritance*,

the Government's White Paper on the Environment.
  Friends of the Earth, September 1990. £6.00

COUNTRYSIDE AND AGRICULTURE

*The Peat Report*
A detailed study of peatbogs as a resource – their use, destruction and the alternatives to the use of peat in gardening.
  Friends of the Earth, March 1990. L102 £4.50

*Peat*
The environmental diversity and richness of peatbogs.
  Friends of the Earth, April 1990. L44 £0.50

*Countryside and Agriculture*
Visual and informative leaflet which explores the environmental issues affecting our countryside.
  Friends of the Earth, August 1990. T107 £0.50

*Sites of Special Scientific Interest*
A detailed account of the damage to Sites of Special Scientific Interest in Britain and the failure of the 1981 Wildlife and Countryside Act.
  Friends of the Earth, July 1984. L45 £2.50

AIR POLLUTION

*Pollution from Diesel Vehicles* by Claire Holman
A report covering the environmental impact and health problems of diesel emissions.
  Friends of the Earth, September 1990. T20 £5.00

*Air Quality and Health* by Claire Holman
A report covering the links between air pollution and health.
  Friends of the Earth, August 1989. T21 £6.00

*Use of CFCs in Buildings* by Curwell, Fox & March
A report on CFCs in the construction industry.
 Fernshaw, December 1988. L23 £12.00

*Safe as Houses*
An abstract of the *Use of CFCs in Buildings* report.
 Friends of the Earth, January 1989. L24 £5.00

*Towards Ozone Friendly Buildings*
How companies are rising to the challenge of eliminating
ozone damaging chemicals.
 Friends of the Earth, March 1990. L26 £6.00

*Coming Clean: Industrial Solvents and the Ozone Layer*
A comprehensive survey of ozone destroying solvents, and
the pros and cons of their alternatives.
 Friends of the Earth, June 1990. L101 £11.00

*Funding Change: Developing Countries and the Montreal
Protocol*
An examination of the problems facing developing
countries when phasing out ozone destroying chemicals.
 Friends of the Earth, 1990. £6.00

BRIEFINGS £0.30 each

*Fridges and CFCs.* L12
*The Effects of Ozone Depletion.* L13
*The Science of Ozone Depletion.* L14
*Particulate Pollution from Diesel Vehicles.* T15
*Cutting Pollution from Petrol Engines.* L16
*Air Quality.* L17
*Lead Pollution.* T18
*Motoring and the Environment.* T19
*Industrial Solvents and the Ozone Layer.* L100
*Methyl Chloroform – Ozone Destroyer.* L102

*'H'CFCs: The Chemical Industry's New Ozone Destroyers.*
L103
*The Catalyst Connection.*

WATER POLLUTION AND WASTE DISPOSAL
BRIEFINGS £0.30 each

*Sitting on a Pollution Timebomb?* (on waste disposal) L46
*Lead in Water.* L48
*Toxic Tips Report.* L49
*Toxic Blue-Green Algae.*

CONSUMER, LOCAL GOVERNMENT, INNER CITIES AND
TRANSPORT ISSUES

*Beyond Green Consumerism*
A pamphlet on Friends of the Earth's view of green
consumerism.
    Friends of the Earth, September 1989. L5 £2.00

*The Environmental Charter for Local Government*
Includes practical recommendations for improving local
government policies and practices.
    Friends of the Earth, November 1989. L6 £13.00

*Action for People*
An appraisal of Government inner city policy.
    Friends of the Earth, March 1989. L7 £5.00

*Reviving the City* by Elkin and McLaren, with Hillman
Towards sustainable urban development.
    Friends of the Earth in association with the Policy
Studies Institute, October 1990. £12.95

*Environmental Audits of Local Authorities: Terms of Reference*
Guidelines to local authorities on how to conduct an

222

environmental audit.
    Friends of the Earth, June 1990. L8 £1.00

*An Illustrated Guide to Traffic Calming: The Future Way of Managing Traffic*
A colour guide explaining how traffic speeds can be controlled by traffic calming measures to benefit the urban environment.
    Friends of the Earth, January 1990. T40 £5.00

*Wheels Within Wheels* by Mick Hamer
A study of the road lobby.
    Friends of the Earth, 1987. L41 £4.00

*Pro-Bike*
A cycling policy for the 1990s.
    Friends of the Earth, 1988. L42 £1.50

*The A-Z of Local Pollution*
How to combat pollution in your own neighbourhood.
    Friends of the Earth, January 1988. T28 £1.00

*Finding Sponsors for Community Projects*
A practical guide.
    Friends of the Earth, April 1990. T4 £3.50

BRIEFINGS £0.30 each

*Green Consumerism.* L110
*Roads to Ruin.* L33
*Roads to Prosperity?* L34
*Heavy Lorries.* L35
*Road and Pavement Maintenance.* L36
*What is PUSWA?* (Public Utilities and Streetworks Act). L37
*Traffic Calming in Residential Areas.* T39

RECYCLING

*Recycling Information*
The basic issues surrounding recycling.
   Friends of the Earth, April 1990. T90 £0.50

*Market Barriers to Paper Recycling*
Research into the use of low grade waste paper by the paper
industry.
   Friends of the Earth, February 1990. L91 £7.00

*Paperchase: A Guide to Office Paper Collection*
How to set up a scheme.
   Friends of the Earth, April 1990. T92 £2.00

*Recycling City – A Partnership for the Future*
The background to 'Recycling City', a project establishing
four model recycling cities in the UK and promoting
recycling throughout the country.
   Friends of the Earth, June 1989. T93 £3.00

*Recycling City Blue Box Information Pack*
A briefing pack on the door-to-door collection of recyclable
materials in Sheffield, a 'Recycling City' project.
   Friends of the Earth, January 1990. T94 £2.50

*Recycling: The Way Forward*
An information pack explaining recycling, with facts and
figures and useful addresses.
   Friends of the Earth, April 1990. T95 £2.50

BRIEFINGS £0.30 each

*Making Recycled Paper*. T83
*Market Barriers to Paper Recycling*. L84
*Setting up a Can Collection*. T87
*Setting up a Paper Collection*. T88

*Getting a Bottle Bank into the Community.* T89
*List of Recycled Paper Wholesalers.* T110

ENERGY

*Getting out of the Greenhouse*
An agenda for action on UK energy policy.
Friends of the Earth, December 1989. L55 £3.00

*Developing Wind Energy for the UK*
A report examining planning issues associated with wind
energy.
Friends of the Earth, January 1990. L54 £3.50.

*Setting Standards for Energy Efficiency*
Making a start on environmental protection.
Friends of the Earth, October 1989. L60 £1.50

*The End of the Nuclear Dream* by Dr Michael Flood
The rise and fall of the UK Atomic Energy Authority, a
critique of its failings and recommendations for its future.
Friends of the Earth, July 1988. L67 £6.00

*Magnox – the Reckoning* by Philip Davies
A detailed economic and safety critique of the magnox
reactor.
Friends of the Earth, August 1988. T66 £2.50

*Unacceptable Levels*
A report on the Sellafield contamination of the River Esk.
Friends of the Earth, October 1989. L56 £4.50

*Fallout over Chernobyl*
A review of the UK's official monitoring programme.
Friends of the Earth, L57 £1.00

*Critical Decision: Should Britain buy the PWR?*
A report on the Sizewell inquiry.
Friends of the Earth, 1986. T63 £2.00

*Good Food Doesn't Need Irradiating*
A briefing paper on food irradiation.
Friends of the Earth, Parents for Safe Food and the London Food Commission, March 1990. T61 £1.50

*Energy*
Visual information leaflet which outlines the environmental aspects of energy use and production.
Friends of the Earth, August 1990. T106 £0.50

BRIEFINGS £0.30 each

*Answering Back: Dealing with difficult questions on energy issues.* L53

TROPICAL RAINFORESTS

*Financing Ecological Disaster: The World Bank and the International Monetary Fund*
Friends of the Earth, September 1988. L76 £2.00

*The Good Wood Guide*
A consumer guide to sustainably managed timber.
Friends of the Earth, January 1990. L81 £5.00

*The Good Wood Manual*
Technical Information on alternatives to tropical timber for architects, designers and the building trade.
Friends of the Earth, January 1990. L82 £41.95

*Timber Trade*
Logging and its effects on the rainforests and tribal peoples.
Friends of the Earth, April 1990. L72 £0.50

*Tropical Rainforests*
Visual and informative leaflet which explains the environmental impact of the destruction of the world's rainforests.
  Friends of the Earth, August 1990. T107 £0.50

BRIEFINGS £0.30 each

*Tropical Rainforests and Third World Debt.* L69
*The Tropical Forestry Action Plan.* L70
*European Community and Tropical Forests.* L71

LEAFLETS FOR 12-18 YEAR OLDS. £0.50 each
Include suggestions for projects.

*Air Pollution.* T105
*Energy.* T106
*Tropical Rainforests* T108
*Water Pollution.* T107

FACT SHEETS FOR CHILDREN, 5-11 YEARS. £0.15 each

Information sheets which aim to introduce younger children to a variety of environmental issues.

| | |
|---|---|
| *Acid Rain* | *Greenhouse Effect* |
| *Agriculture* | *Ozone Depletion* |
| *Air Pollution* | *Recycling* |
| *Energy* | *Water* |

OTHER SOURCES OF INFORMATION:

Amos, Chris, 1989. *A Testing time for new settlements?* Town and Country Planning, Volume 58, pp. 314–319.
Association of Metropolitan Authorities 1990. *Bus Deregulation: The Metropolitan Experience.* London, AMA.
Bardos P and others, 1990. *Market Barriers to Materials Reclamation and Recycling.* Department of Trade and Industry, Warren Spring Laboratory.

Cabinet Office. *Annual Review of Government Funded Research and Development*. London, HMSO.

Civic Trust 1989. *Urban Wasteland Now*. London, Civic Trust.

Department of Energy 1989. *Digest of United Kingdom Energy Statistics*. London, HMSO.

Department of the Environment 1988. *A review of derelict land policy*. London, HMSO.

Department of the Environment 1988. *An evaluation of the Urban Development Programme*. London, HMSO.

Department of the Environment 1989. *Her Majesty's Inspectorate of Pollution Report 1987–88*. London, HMSO.

Department of the Environment 1989. *Inner City Programmes 1987–88*. London, DoE.

Department of the Environment 1990. *Digest of Environmental Protection and Water Statistics, No. 12, 1989*. London, HMSO.

Department of the Environment. *Land Use Change in England*. Annual Statistical Bulletins. London, DoE.

Department of Trade and Industry 1990. *CFCs and Halons*. London, HMSO.

Department of Transport 1989. *Roads to Prosperity* (White Paper on Transport). London, HMSO.

Docklands Consultative Committee 1987. *Six Year Review of the London Docklands Development Corporation*. London, DCC.

House of Commons Agriculture Committee 1990. *Bovine Spongiform Encephalopathy (BSE)*. London, HMSO.

House of Commons Energy Committee 1988. *The Structure, Regulation and Economic Consequences of Electricity Supply in the Private Sector*. London, HMSO.

House of Commons Energy Committee 1989. *Energy Policy Implications of the Greenhouse Effect*. London, HMSO.

House of Commons Energy Committee 1990. *The Cost of Nuclear Power*. London, HMSO.

House of Commons Environment Committee 1984. *Acid Rain*. London, HMSO.

House of Commons Official Report. *Parliamentary Debates* (Hansard). London, HMSO.

House of Lords Select Committee on Science and Technology 1981. *Hazardous Waste Disposal*. London, HMSO.

House of Lords Select Committee on the European Communities 1989. *Efficiency Of Electricity Use*. London, HMSO.

International Tropical Timber Organisation 1988. *Annual Report*. Japan, ITTO.

London Regional Transport 1990. *Annual Report and Accounts 1989/1990*. London, LRT.

Nature Conservancy Council 1989. *Fifteenth Report*. Peterborough, Nature Conservancy Council.

Paris Commission 1989. *Tenth Annual Report*. London, Paris Commission.

Pearce D, Markandya A, Barbier EB 1989. *Blueprint for a Green Economy* ('The Pearce Report'). London, Earthscan.

Sherlock, H, 1990. *Cities are Good for Us*. London, Transport 2000.

Third North Sea Conference 1990. *1990 Interim Report on the Quality Status of the North Sea*. Department of Transport and Public Works, The Hague, The Netherlands.

*This Common Inheritance* (White Paper on the Environment) (1990). London, HMSO.

Welsh Affairs Select Committee 1990. *Toxic Waste Disposal in Wales*. London, HMSO.

World Commission on Environment and Development 1987. *Our Common Future* ('The Brundtland Report'). Oxford, Oxford University Press.

# ABOUT FRIENDS OF THE EARTH

**Friends of the Earth Ltd** is one of the leading environmental pressure groups in the UK. We blow the whistle on those who destroy the environment, and put pressure on those who have the power to protect it. We are backed by more than 200,000 supporters and represent the concerns and interests of many thousands of people.

We work with all political parties, but are aligned to none. We have an impressive reputation for giving 'early warnings' of environmental hazards – but politicians rarely act until public pressure forces them to. Friends of the Earth exists to mobilise that pressure for change.

*Locally:* Friends of the Earth has a network of about 300 Local Groups across the country and more than 80 Earth Action Groups for young people aged 14 to 23.

*Funding:* Most of our income comes from our supporters. The rest comes from special fundraising events, grants and trading.

**Friends of the Earth Trust** is a charity which commissions detailed research and provides extensive information material to enable everyone to do their bit for the environment.

*The Projects Unit:* The Projects Unit provides practical support to environmental projects throughout the UK. Funded by UK2000, it has five full-time staff.

*The Arts for the Earth:* The Arts for the Earth (TATE)

was set up to strengthen the ties between the environmental movement and those involved in all aspects of the arts.

**Friends of the Earth International** is a network of independent national groups in 38 countries, with an International Secretariat based in London.

# The Earth needs all the friends it can get.
# And it needs them now.

For thousands upon thousands of years our planet has sustained a rich diversity of life. Now, one single species – humankind – is putting the Earth at risk.

People the world over are suffering the effects of pollution, deforestation and radiation. Species are disappearing at a terrifying rate. The warming of the atmosphere threatens us all with devastating change in climate and food production.

But it needn't be like this – we know enough to reverse the damage, and to manage the Earth's wealth more fairly and sustainably. But the political will to bring about such a transformation is still lacking.

And that's exactly where Friends of the Earth comes in.

## IT'S TIME YOU JOINED US

I'd like to join Friends of the Earth. Please send me your quarterly magazine. I enclose:

£12 ☐ individual  £17 ☐ family  £250 ☐ life

I'd like to donate  £50 ☐  £35 ☐  £15 ☐

Other £ _____

I enclose a cheque/PO for total of £_____
payable to **Friends of the Earth** or debit my Access/Visa No:

_____

Card expiry date: _____

Signature _____  Date _____

FULL NAME _____

ADDRESS _____

_____

_____

_____  POSTCODE _____

Send to: Membership Dept, Friends of the Earth, FREEPOST, 56–58 Alma Street, Luton, Beds LU1 2YZ

**081 200 0200 to join/donate anytime**

Friends of the Earth

**F81 LACZ**

# Index

Local Government, Planning and
Land Act 1980 106–7
London County Council 97
London Docklands Development
Corporation
London Ecology Unit 108
London Planning Advisory
Committee 116
London Regional Transport 127,
129
Luxembourg 6

Major, John 123
Marine Conservation Society 18
Marshall (Lord) 47
MCA (Music Corporation of
America) 8
mercury 16, 20, 33
methane 149, 157
methyl chloroform 10, 169, 174
Minerals Act 1981 91
Ministry of Agriculture, Fisheries
& Food (MAFF) 20, 30, 49,
61, 71, 78, 113, 180
Montreal Protocol 10

National Audit Office 73, 125
National Council for Voluntary
Organisations 163
National Economic Development
Office 66
National Federation of Housing
Associations 100
National Radiological Protection
Board 52
National Rivers Authority (NRA)
14, 22, 26, 30, 32–3, 82
Natural Environment Research
Council 178, 181–2
Natural History Museum 184, 187
Nature Conservancy Council
(NCC) 21, 71, 75, 76, 87, 88,
91, 93–4, 96, 198
Netherlands 3, 6, 65, 123, 124,
147, 159, 214

Newton, Tony 170
Nicholson, Max 93
NIREX 50
nitrate 20–22
nitrate sensitive areas 22
nitric oxide 1
nitrogen dioxide 1, 8, 9
nitrogen fertiliser 69, 77
nitrogen oxides (NOx) 1, 4, 6, 11
nitrous oxide 203, 206
Norfolk Broads 61
North Sea
waste dumping 15
nitrate 16
oil 55
phosphate 16
pollution 15–17
research 183
sewage 15
North Sea Conference 16, 19, 31
Norway 3, 214
nuclear power 46–53

Office of Electricity Regulation 46
organic farming 71
Organisation for Economic Co-
operation and Development
192
Oslo Commission 15
overseas aid 191–4
Overseas Development
Administration 191, 195, 196,
199, 201
Oxleas Wood 125
ozone 1, 8
ozone layer 2, 10–11, 179
and carbon tetrachloride 10
and CFCs 10, 11
and halons 10
and HCFCs
(hydrochlorofluorocarbons) 10
and methyl chloroform 10

Parents for Safe Food 80–1

agriculture 180
Ridley, Nicholas x, 73, 98, 116,
    121, 124, 127, 131, 182
Ripa di Meana, Carlo 214
river pollution 20, 82
roads
    injuries 123
    planning 123
    public inquiries 130–1
    building programmes 121, 123–
    4, 133
    lorry weights 125–6
Royal Commission on
    Environmental Pollution
    (RCEP) 9, 30, 135, 140, 153
Royal Institute of British Architects
    42
Royal Mail Letters 127
Royal Society for Nature
    Conservation 91
Royal Society for the Protection of
    Birds 74, 87, 91
Royal Town Planning Institute 116
Ryder, Richard 162

Sarawak 197–8
Sea Mammal Research Unit 181
Scottish Office 75–6
Secretary of State for the
    Environment 16, 97
Sellafield 49, 50, 51, 59
sewage sludge 16, 19
sewage treatment 16, 19, 27
    effluent standards 19, 28
    outfalls 18
Shell 82
Simplified Planning Zones 106
Sites of Special Scientific Interest
    90
    damage 65, 87, 90–2, 118, 125
    Dover Cliffs 88
    Flow Country 75
    Foxley Wood 98
    Gwenlais valley 93

Mersey Estuary 87
    payments 90–1
    planning permission 91
    Poole Harbour 56
    Rainham Marshes 88–9
    Thorne Moors 92
    Tiger Bay 101
    Twyford Down 88, 125
soil erosion 60, 70
Soil Survey 60, 70
Southwood Committee 62
Special Development Orders 114–
    15
Special Protection Areas 87
Squire, Robin 115
structure plans 115
sulphur dioxide ($SO_2$) 1, 3–5, 41,
    137
Sweden 3, 6, 11, 39, 42, 65, 214
Switzerland 65

Thatcher, Margaret ix, x, xiii, 5,
    20, 90, 177, 192, 194, 205,
    208, 210, 211–13
Thorne Moors 92
tidal barrages 87, 101
Trades Description Act 1968 174–6
Transport and Road Research
    Laboratory 128
Tree Preservation Orders 95
Trippier, David 5, 10, 92, 136, 150
Tropical Forestry Action Plan
    (TFAP) 193, 199–200, 210
tropical rainforests 188–202
    and dams 192, 196–7
    and debt 189–90
    deforestation 188
tropical timber
    imports 197, 202, 218
    labelling 199
Twyford Down 88

UK Atomic Energy Authority 54
UN Economic Commission for
    Europe 3

241